children's illustrated encyclopedia

Atlas of the World

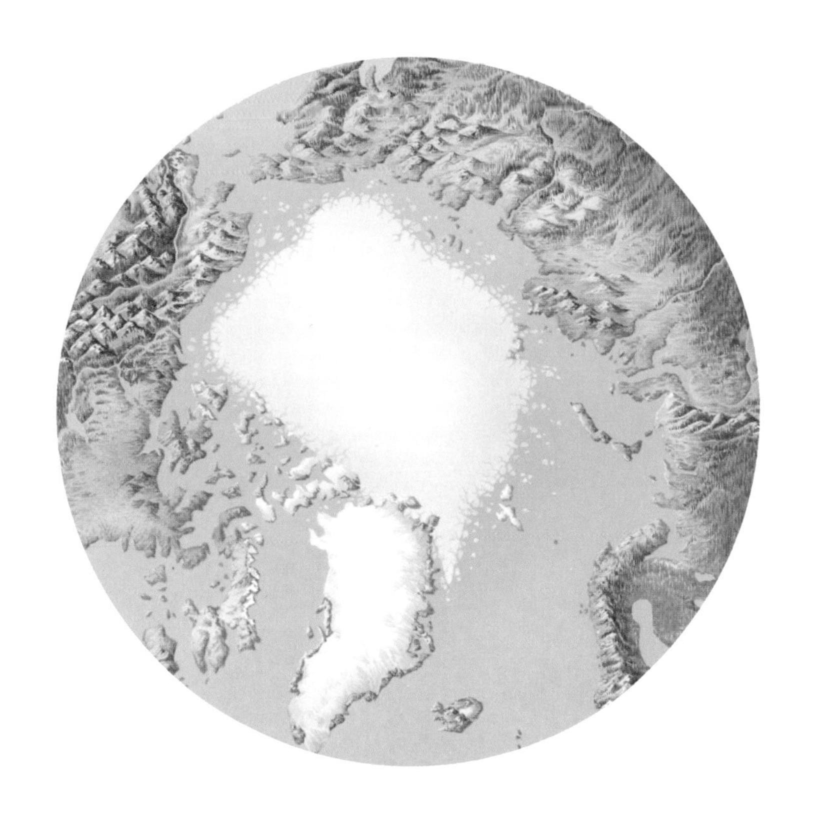

First published in 2009 by Orpheus Books Ltd.,
6 Church Green, Witney, Oxfordshire OX28 4AW England
www.orpheusbooks.com

Created and produced by Orpheus Books Ltd

Text Claire Aston

Illustrators Gary Hincks, Steve Noon

Map on pages 4-5: Olive Pearson

ISBN 978 1 905473 44 1

A CIP record for this book is available from the British Library.

Printed and bound in Singapore

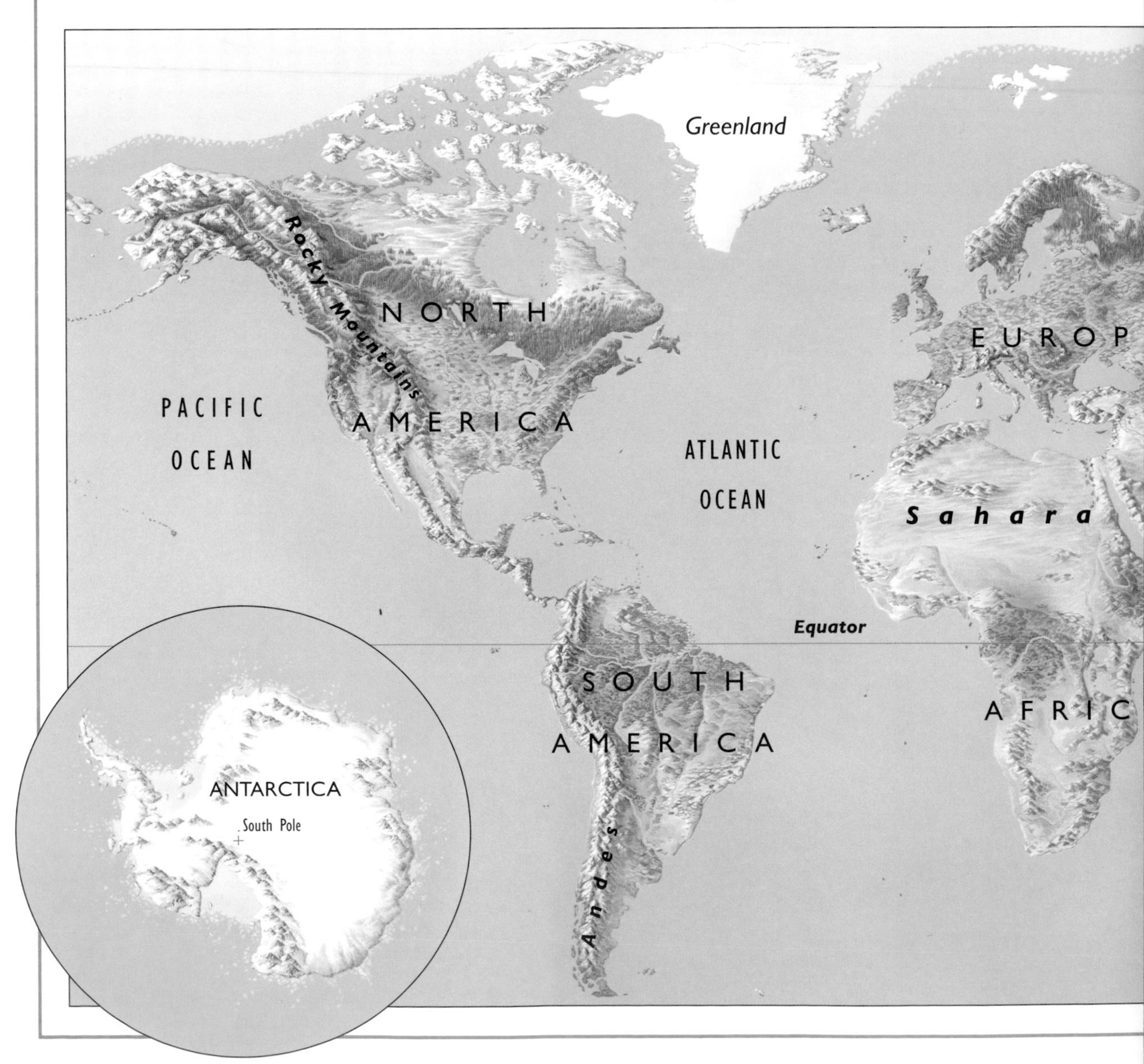

CONTENTS

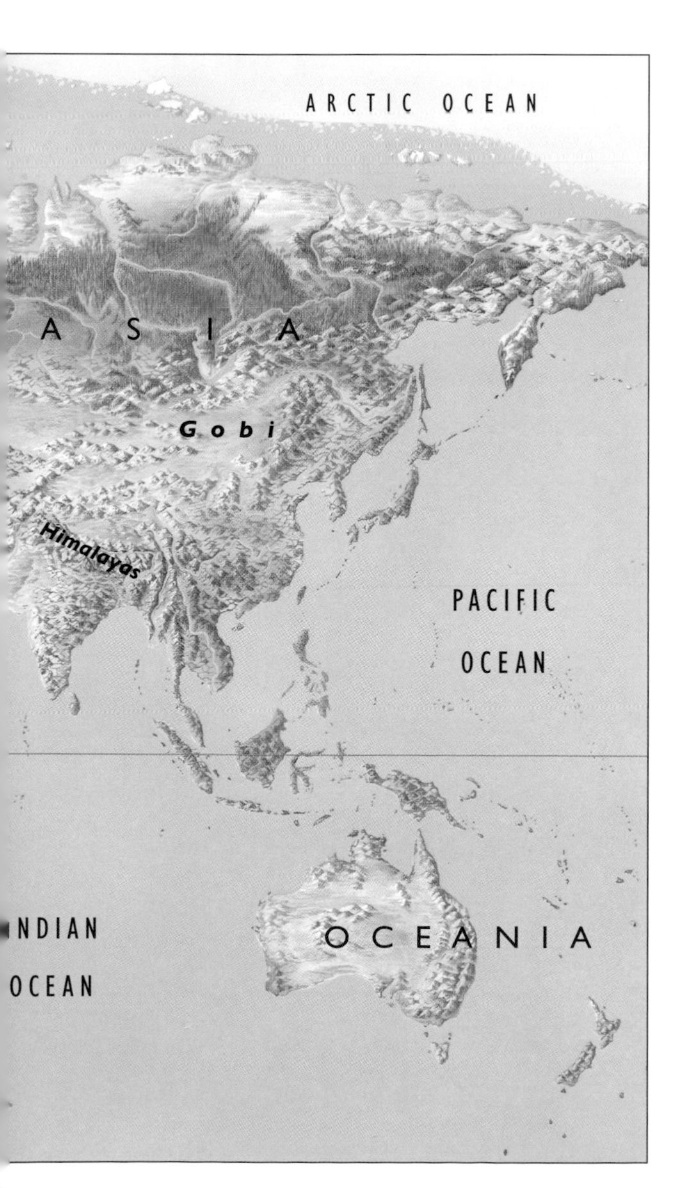
ARCTIC OCEAN
ASIA
Gobi
Himalayas
PACIFIC OCEAN
INDIAN OCEAN
OCEANIA

UNITED STATES OF AMERICA

THE UNITED STATES of America stretches from the Atlantic Ocean in the east to the Pacific Ocean in the west. Numbered among its 50 states are Alaska, which lies to the northwest of Canada, and the Pacific islands of Hawaii.

Running down the northeastern side of the USA are the densely-forested Appalachian Mountains. To their northwest lie the Great Lakes, vast inland seas that were gouged out by glaciers during the Ice Ages and filled by their meltwaters. To the east lie the coastal lowlands, where great cities such as New York, Boston and Washington have grown up.

The famous symbol of San Francisco, the Golden Gate bridge spans the entrance to San Francisco bay. It carries cars and pedestrians for 2.7 km across the water.

Covering the central belt of the USA is a vast, flat area of farmland. In the northern part, crops such as wheat and maize are grown, while cotton, tobacco and nuts are cultivated further south. The vast Mississippi river cuts through several of the midwestern states, dividing the USA in two.

West of the high Rocky Mountains, the climate is drier, and the landscape more rugged. Wide areas of hot desert stretch across the southwestern states of Nevada and Arizona. Near the west coast, the climate becomes milder. Rich farmland nestles among the mountain ranges of California and the northwestern states.

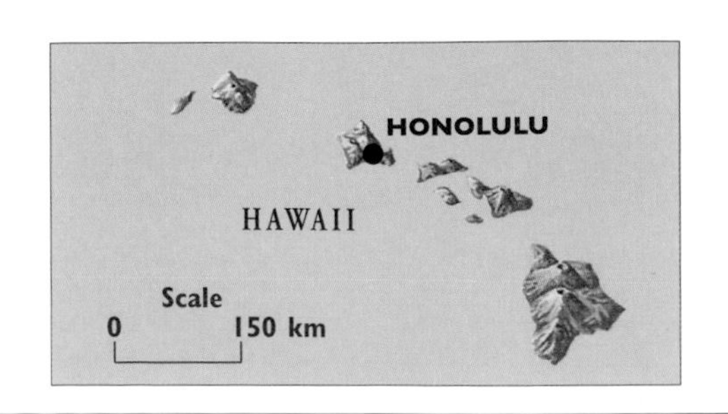

Before the first settlers arrived from Europe, the Native Americans were the only inhabitants of the USA. Today, Americans can trace their ancestors from all parts of the world. Many black Americans are the descendents of slaves brought over from Africa in the 17th and 18th centuries.

New Orleans, in the southern state of Louisiana, is the home of jazz and blues music. This came from the songs of the early black population. The city was devastated in 2005 by Hurricane Katrina.

The Gateway Arch stands on the bank of the Mississippi river in St. Louis, Missouri. At 192 metres high, it is the highest monument in the world. It was built in 1965, to symbolize the "Gateway to the West". In the 19th century, many people travelled west from St. Louis to begin a new life in Oregon and California.

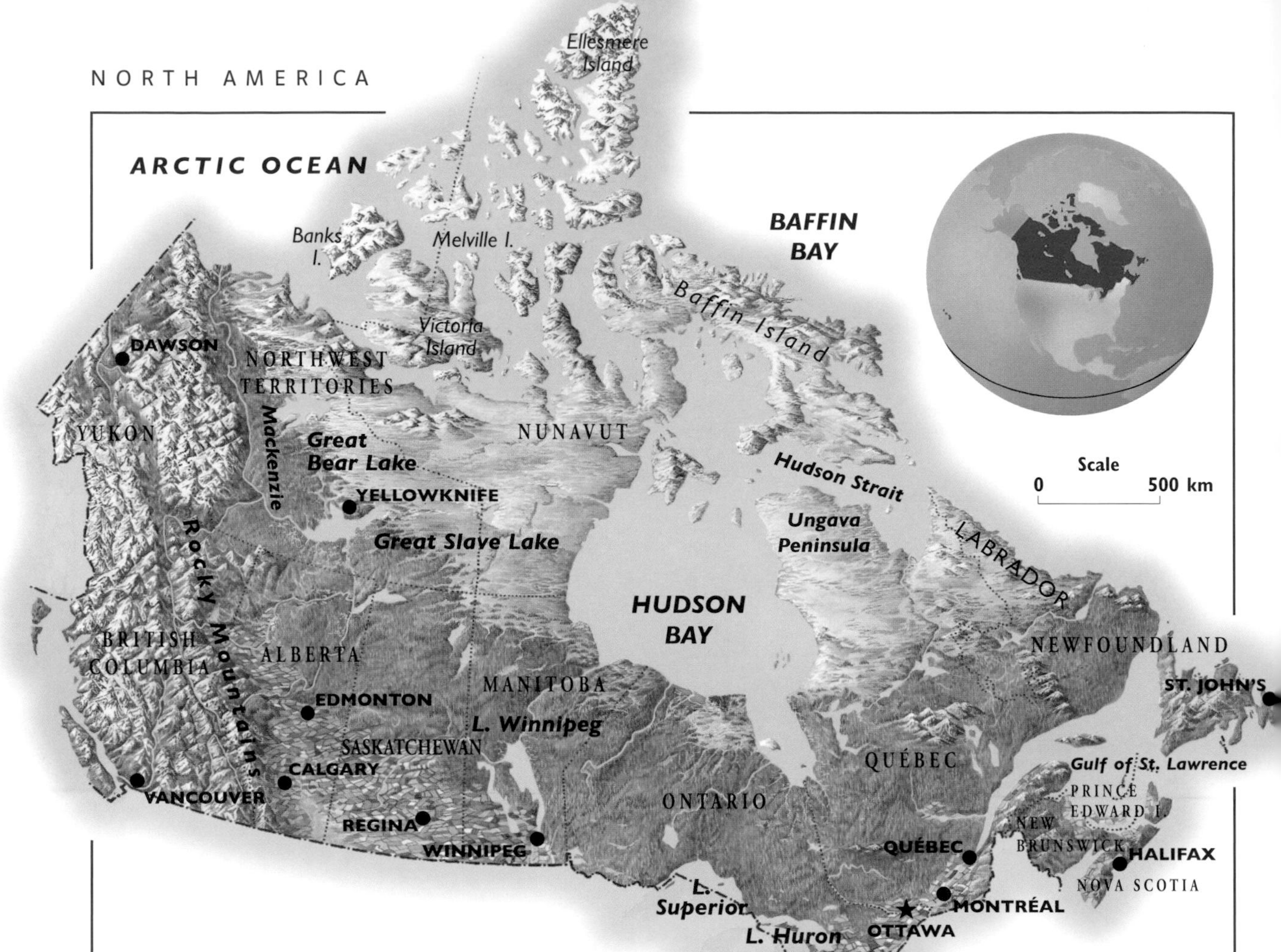

CANADA

ALTHOUGH larger in size than the USA, Canada has a much smaller population than its neighbour. Most of the country is covered with vast coniferous forests, mountains and lakes, where bears, wolves, cougars and moose are abundant. In the far north, and on the Arctic islands, the ground is permanently frozen. On this barren land, known as the tundra, plants grow only in the short summer.

Some native peoples, including the Inuit, live in the icy northern territories, but most Canadians live in the south, near the border with the USA. The largest cities are located in the east. Further west, in the provinces of Alberta, Saskatchewan and Manitoba, lies a wide expanse of fertile, low-lying land known as the Great Plains, or prairies, where most of Canada's wheat crop is grown. The western part of Canada is dominated by mountain ranges, including the Rocky Mountains, which stretch on south across the USA.

Grain from the fertile prairies is stored in grain elevators before being distributed around Canada and abroad.

In the 16th century, the first European settlers arrived in Canada from both France and Great Britain. French and English are still the official languages spoken today. Most French-speaking Canadians live in the province of Québec, and many wish to see it declared a separate country.

Mexico and Central America

MEXICO and the countries that make up Central America form a link between North and South America. Mexico is a mountainous country, with desert in the north, tropical forest in the south and a central plateau of fertile land. Its cities suffer from overcrowding and pollution.

Central America is a mainly agricultural area. Bananas and coffee are grown, and cattle are raised. There is a constant threat of volcanoes, earthquakes and hurricanes.

The first European settlers of this region were Spanish. They controlled the land for hundreds of years. Most Mexicans and Central Americans speak Spanish today.

This volcano, Arenal, rises from the rain-forest of Costa Rica.

Rice winnowing on Haiti *(below)*. The rice is sieved to remove the grain from the outer husks.

Caribbean Islands

The beautiful islands of the Caribbean are popular tourist resorts. They also export crops such as sugar, bananas and coffee. Volcanic eruptions and frequent hurricanes are a constant threat to the islanders.
Many Caribbean people are descended from black African slaves. Their cultures are a mixture of African and European traditions.

South America

VENEZUELA, the Guianas (Guyana, Surinam and French Guiana) and Brazil are rich in natural resources such as oil, bauxite, silver and other minerals. Brazil also produces coffee, sugar and fruit for export, while Guyana has large sugar plantations. Despite these resources, there is a great contrast in the distribution of wealth. A few people are very rich, while others live in poverty. The towns and cities are densely populated with people looking for work. Clusters of poor housing known as shantytowns, built from whatever materials can be found, sprawl around the edges of cities such as Rio de Janeiro and São Paulo.

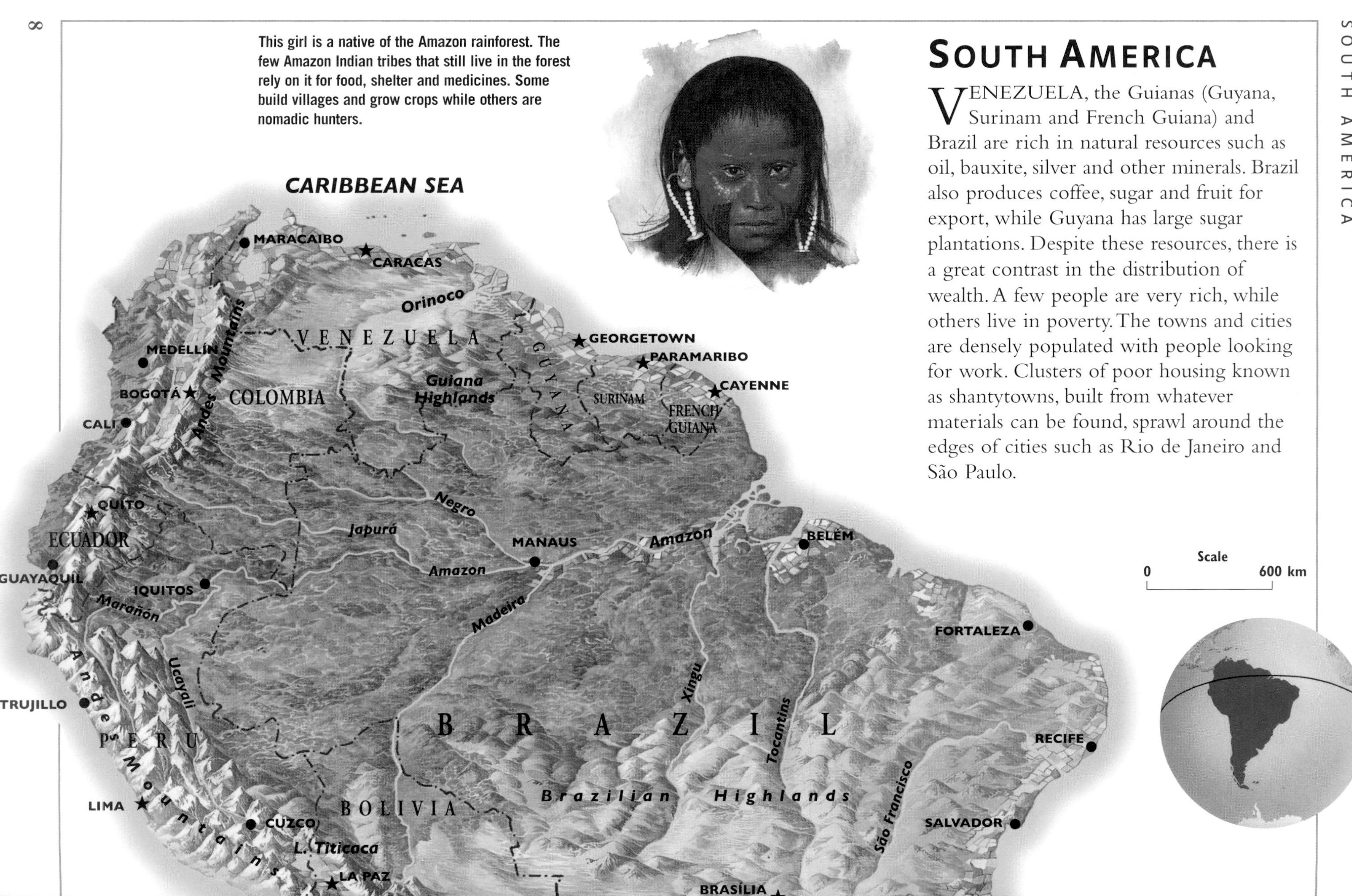

This girl is a native of the Amazon rainforest. The few Amazon Indian tribes that still live in the forest rely on it for food, shelter and medicines. Some build villages and grow crops while others are nomadic hunters.

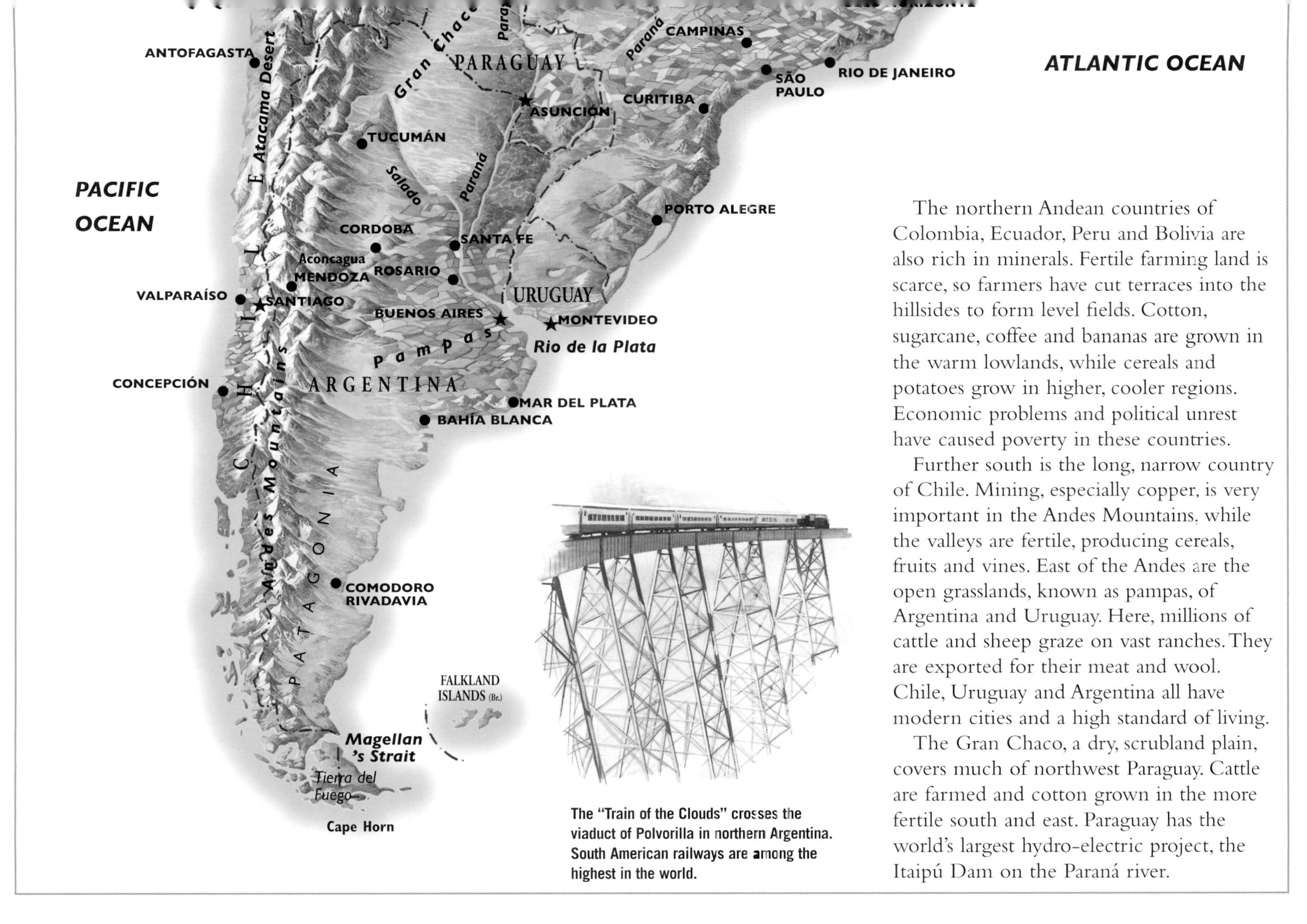

The "Train of the Clouds" crosses the viaduct of Polvorilla in northern Argentina. South American railways are among the highest in the world.

The northern Andean countries of Colombia, Ecuador, Peru and Bolivia are also rich in minerals. Fertile farming land is scarce, so farmers have cut terraces into the hillsides to form level fields. Cotton, sugarcane, coffee and bananas are grown in the warm lowlands, while cereals and potatoes grow in higher, cooler regions. Economic problems and political unrest have caused poverty in these countries.

Further south is the long, narrow country of Chile. Mining, especially copper, is very important in the Andes Mountains, while the valleys are fertile, producing cereals, fruits and vines. East of the Andes are the open grasslands, known as pampas, of Argentina and Uruguay. Here, millions of cattle and sheep graze on vast ranches. They are exported for their meat and wool. Chile, Uruguay and Argentina all have modern cities and a high standard of living.

The Gran Chaco, a dry, scrubland plain, covers much of northwest Paraguay. Cattle are farmed and cotton grown in the more fertile south and east. Paraguay has the world's largest hydro-electric project, the Itaipú Dam on the Paraná river.

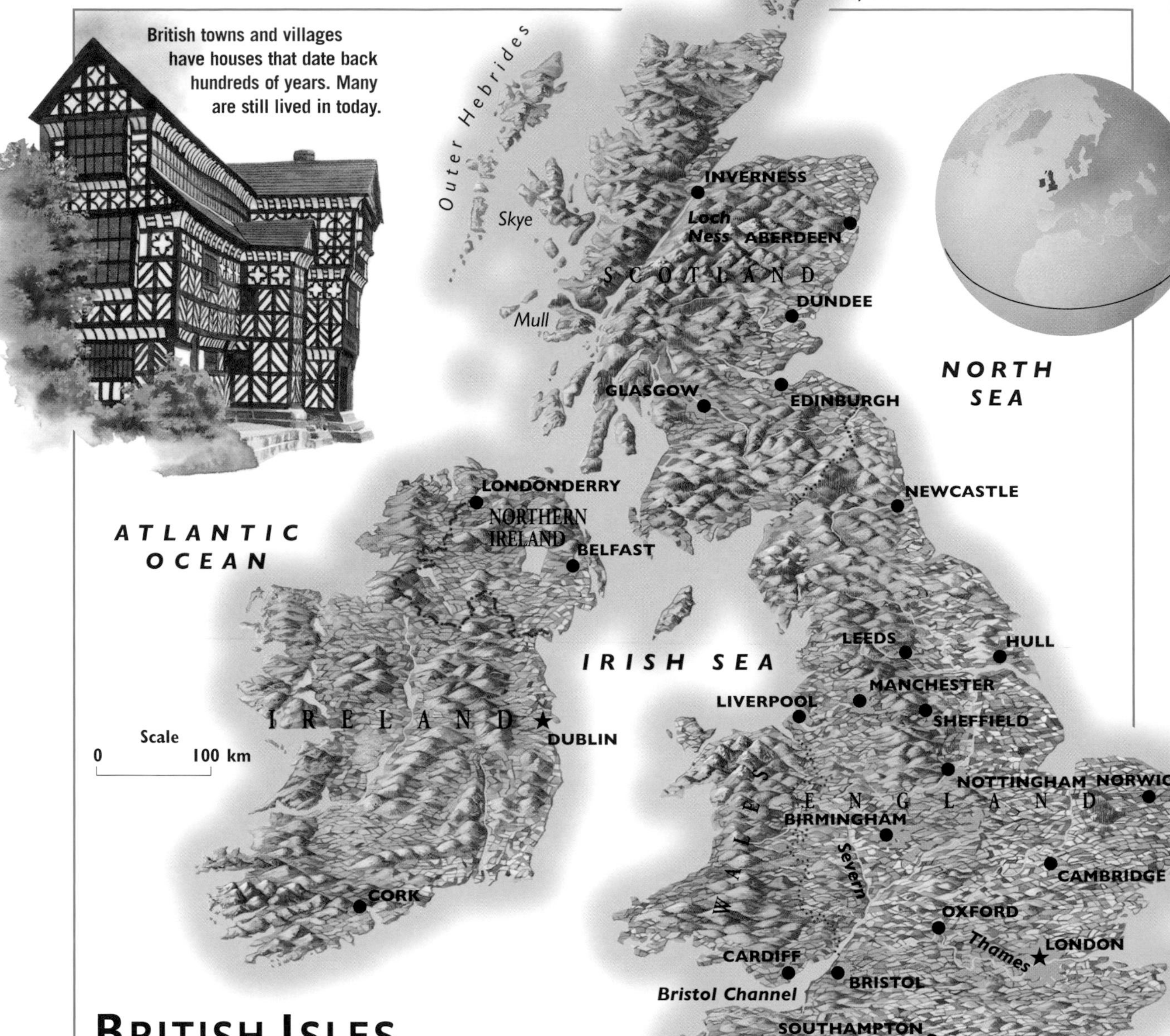

British Isles

THE BRITISH ISLES includes the large islands of Great Britain and Ireland, and many smaller islands. England, Scotland, Wales and Northern Ireland make up the United Kingdom. The rest of Ireland became independent in 1922. For many years conflict has divided the Catholic and Protestant people of Northern Ireland.

Mountains dominate the sparsely populated north of Scotland. Northern England and Wales also have large areas of uplands. Central and southern England are a dense mix of farmland, towns and cities. Because of its mild, wet climate, Ireland is famous for its lush green landscape.

The United Kingdom was once dominated by heavy industries such as coal-mining and shipbuilding. Today, light industry such as plastics manufacture and electronics, as well as communications and financial services, have become important.

Once the hub of a worldwide empire, Britain still plays a leading role in international affairs. Its language, English, is spoken as a second language all over the world, and is dominant on the Internet and other areas of international communication.

FRANCE

FRANCE shares borders with several other countries on its eastern side, but the north and west look on to the sea. In the south, the Pyrenees mountains separate France from Spain, while the Alps form a border with Italy in the east. The Mediterranean Sea gives the south coast its warm climate and makes it a popular destination for tourists.

Much of France, especially in the north, is strongly agricultural. Many large rivers wind across fertile, undulating plains. France exports large quantities of food and wine, famous for its quality. It also has modern manufacturing and chemical industries. Nuclear power provides much of the country's electricity supplies.

Most people in France are descended from ancient peoples including the Gauls, a Central European tribe, and the Franks, after whom the country is named. More recently, people from France's former colonies in North Africa have made their homes in France.

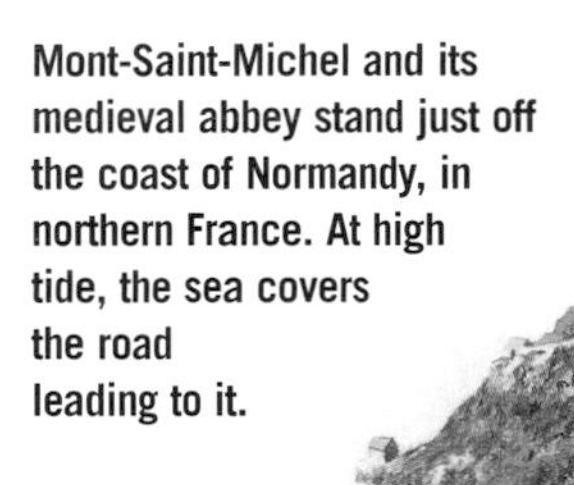

Mont-Saint-Michel and its medieval abbey stand just off the coast of Normandy, in northern France. At high tide, the sea covers the road leading to it.

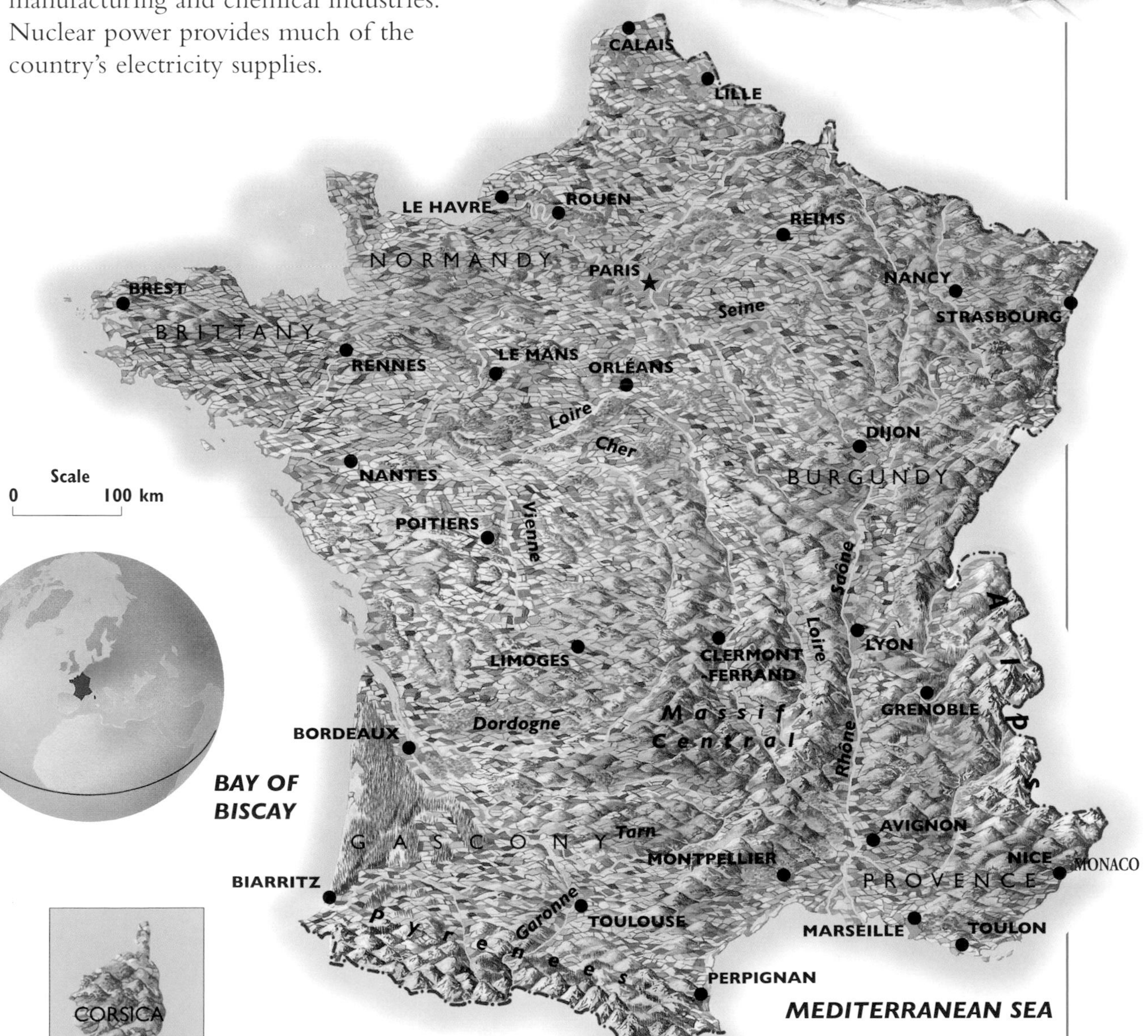

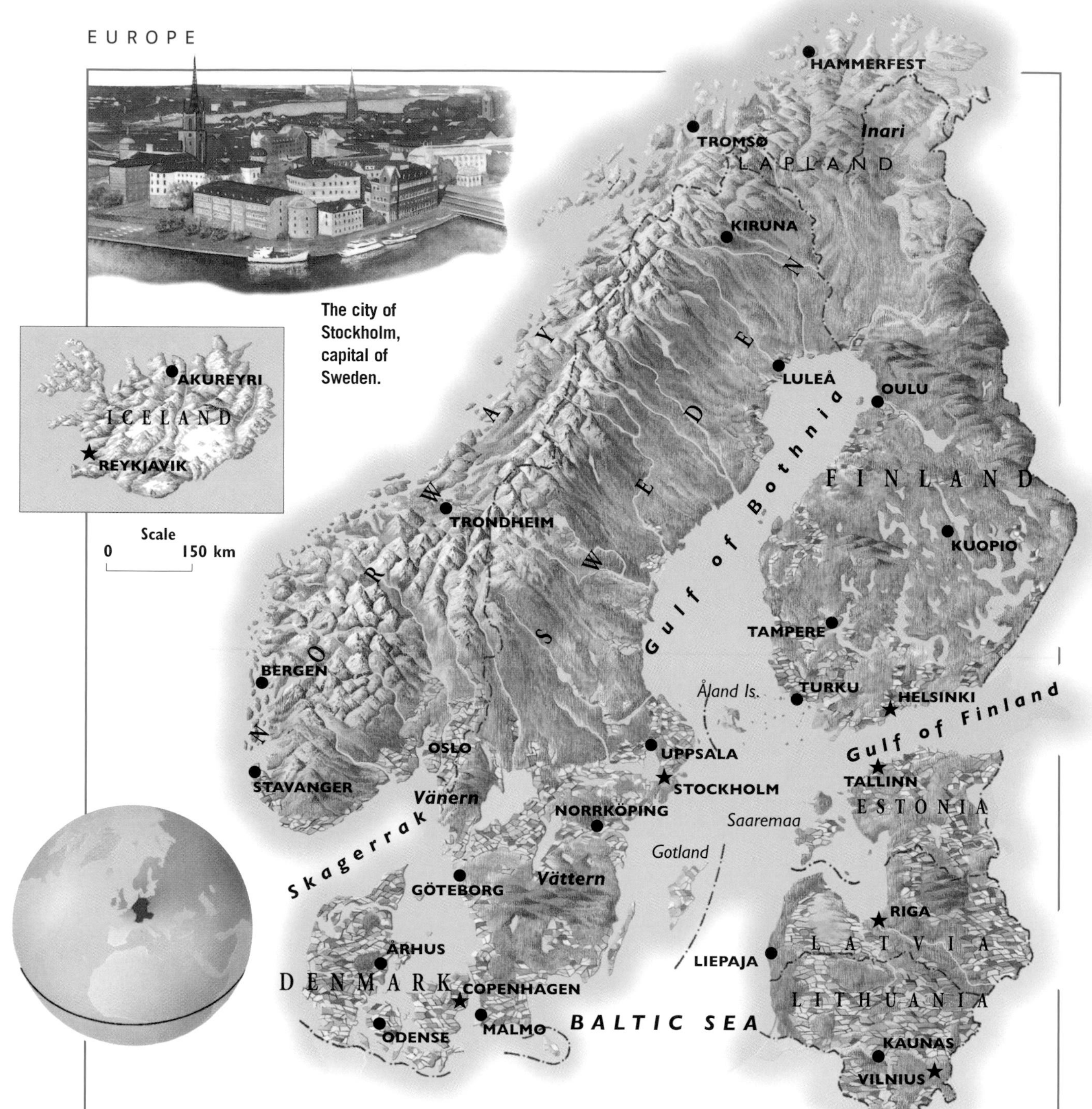

The city of Stockholm, capital of Sweden.

NORTHERN EUROPE

NORWAY, Sweden and Denmark are together known as Scandinavia. Along with Finland and the volcanic island of Iceland, they form the Nordic countries. Some parts of Norway, Sweden and Finland lie within the Arctic Circle, where the sun never sets in high summer, but never rises in the depths of the long, cold winter.

Norway and Sweden are mountainous countries, while Finland and Denmark are low-lying. Finland is covered with dense coniferous forests and many lakes. In the past, glaciers have carved out the many inlets, or fjords, in Norway's coastline.

The Nordic countries are prosperous and have low populations. They are important producers of timber, and are also world leaders in manufacturing. Denmark is also a farming country, with many dairy and pig farms.

The Baltic countries of Estonia, Latvia and Lithuania used to be part of the former Soviet Union. Timber, fishing and farming are their most important industries.

Germany and the Low Countries

At the centre of Europe lies Germany, with its neighbours Austria and Switzerland, and the "low countries" of Belgium, the Netherlands and Luxembourg.

Germany is flat and fertile in the north and heavily forested in the hills of the central and southern areas. It is a wealthy country, and an industrial leader, producing cars, electrical goods and chemicals for export all over the world.

The Alps rise in the south of Germany. Much of the area of Austria and Switzerland is taken up by Alpine peaks and valleys. These picturesque, prosperous countries also have modern industries.

The Brandenburg Gate in Berlin.

The Netherlands is famous for its dairy goods and fields of flowers. Belgium is a land of two regions: the north, Dutch-speaking Flanders, is mostly level farmland, while the south, French-speaking Wallonia is hilly, wooded country.

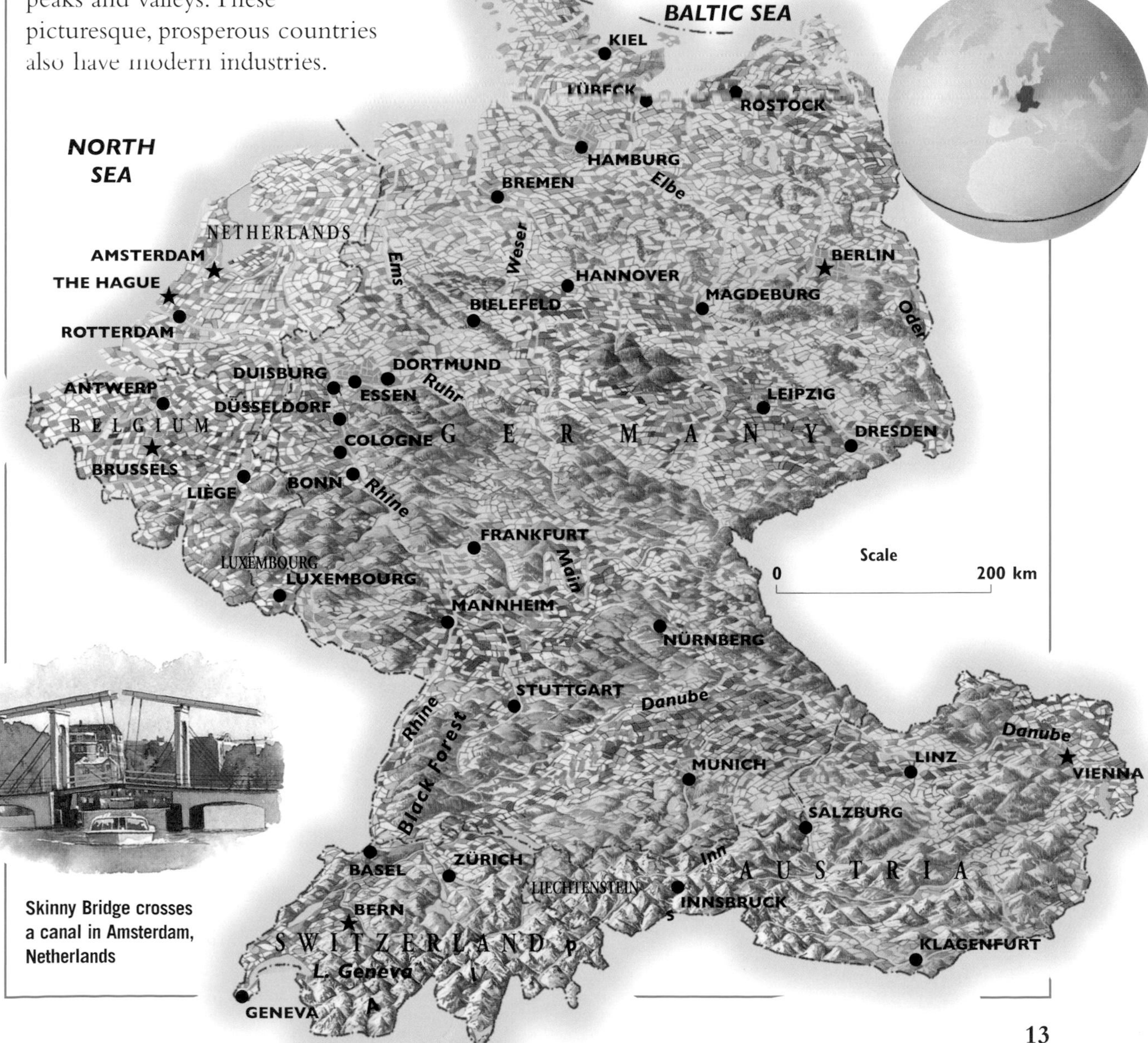

Skinny Bridge crosses a canal in Amsterdam, Netherlands

Spain and Portugal

THE IBERIAN PENINSULA, divided between the countries of Spain and Portugal, is separated from the rest of Europe by the Pyrenees mountains. The core of the peninsula is a plateau called the Meseta, a landscape of plains crossed by several mountain ranges.

Spain has four official languages—Galician, Catalan, Basque as well as Spanish—and several dialects. The north of the country, Spain's industrial heartland, is cooler and wetter. Central Spain is much drier. Large areas are barren or given over to rough pasture for sheep and goats. Tourist resorts have grown up along the Mediterranean coast. Andalucia is famous for bull-fighting, sherry, orange trees and flamenco dancers.

Portugal has long held close ties with the sea. Famous for its explorers, Portuguese sailors founded colonies in Africa, Asia and America more than 500 years ago. Today, farming and fishing are among the main industries—supplying the world with anchovies, sardines, shellfish, cork and port, a sweet wine produced in the region near Porto. Along the drier south coast is the Algarve, popular with tourists.

The Luiz I bridge spans the River Douro at Porto, Northern Portugal.

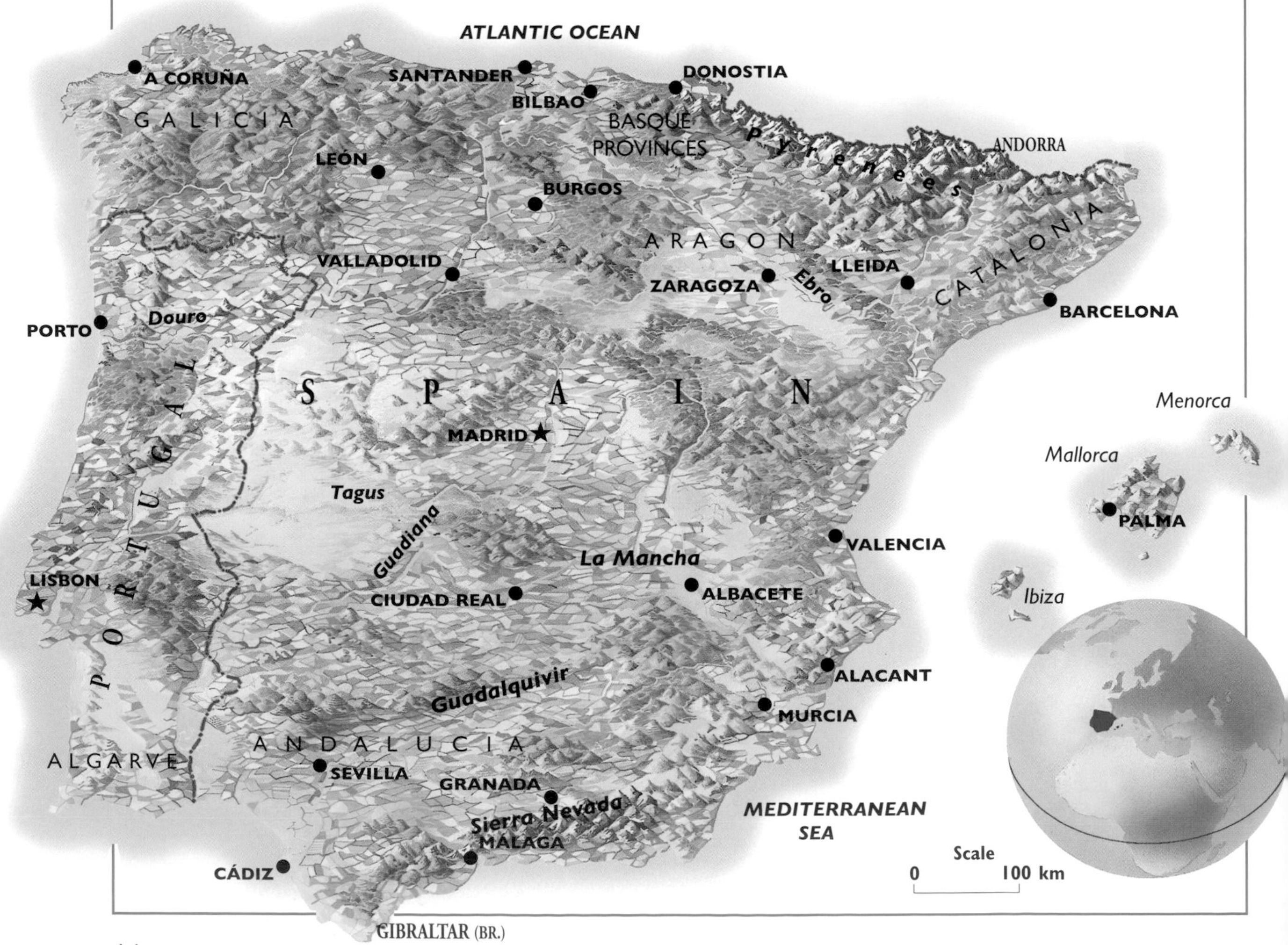

Venice was built on an island in a lagoon. Instead of streets and cars, there are canals and gondolas.

ITALY

SURROUNDED on three sides by the Mediterranean Sea, Italy is shaped like a boot about to kick a stone—the island of Sicily. The Alps, including the jagged, limestone Dolomites, form the border in the north. Running the length of the boot down to the toe are the thickly-wooded Apennines. Both Sicily and Sardinia are rugged, hilly islands.

Italy also has three active volcanoes: Vesuvius, Stromboli and Etna. In AD 79, Vesuvius erupted, burying the town of Pompeii. The remains of a great Roman civilization have since been uncovered.

Northern Italy is more prosperous than the south, Sicily and Sardinia. There are major industrial cities such as Milan and Turin, vineyards, and fields of wheat, maize and tomatoes.

The Vatican City, which lies within the city of Rome, is the smallest independent state in the world. It is home to the Pope, the head of the Catholic church.

CENTRAL AND EASTERN EUROPE

MUCH OF CENTRAL and Eastern Europe is flat, low-lying land. A large part of this is given over to farming, but native forest still remains in upland areas, where elk, wolves and bison roam. The northern part of this region has warm summers but cold winters. Crops such as potatoes and cereals are grown, and animals are farmed for their milk and meat.

Heavy industries such as mining, metal-working, car production and glass-making are important for the economy of Poland. Pollution from the burning of coal to produce electricity, and from factories and cars, threatens the environment.

In the south, the forested Sudetes and Carpathian Mountain ranges rim the Czech Republic and cover much of Slovakia. Cereals, root vegetables and livestock are farmed in the valleys. The fertile lowlands of Hungary are scattered with orchards and vineyards. All three countries have vehicle, chemical and textile industries.

The undulating lowlands of the Ukraine with their fertile "black earth" have long been intensively cultivated. There are fields of wheat, barley, sugar beet and sunflowers. Manufacturing is concentrated in the Ukraine's southeastern cities.

The borders of Central and Eastern Europe have changed many times over the years. Until recently, many countries were controlled by, or were part of the former Soviet Union. They are now independent, and starting to grow in prosperity.

Odesa is a major industrial port on the south coast of the Ukraine. The warm waters of the Black Sea have made this coast a popular destination for tourists.

SOUTHEAST EUROPE

THE BALKANS, which make up most of south-east Europe, are lands of rugged mountains and deep valleys. Winters are cold, but cotton, tobacco and grapes can be grown in the warm summers. Several of these countries were once part of Yugoslavia. The creation of new borders, as well as clashes between ethnic groups, has led to conflict.

Greece is one of the oldest nations in Europe. As a mountainous country, farming space is limited, and its olive groves and vineyards are scattered along the hillsides. Greece has many islands, and a large part of its economy relies on a large shipping industry and tourism.

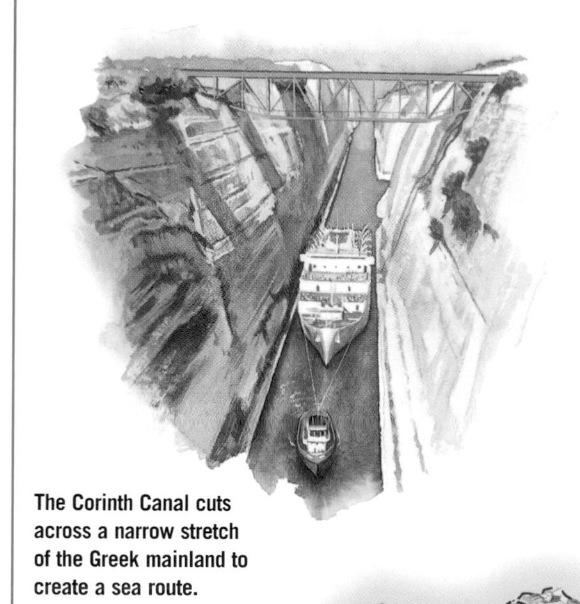

The Corinth Canal cuts across a narrow stretch of the Greek mainland to create a sea route.

Slovenian farm buildings have a wooden frame called a *kozolec* to store hay.

Turkey is split between Europe and Asia by a narrow stretch of water called the Bosporus. Turkey's coasts are warm, but the dry grasslands of its interior can be bitterly cold in winter. Turkey is famous for its craft industry, especially carpets and pottery. Its Mediterranean coastline and ancient sites also make it a popular tourist destination.

RUSSIA

STRETCHING between two continents, Europe and Asia, Russia is the largest country in the world. Until 1991 it was part of the Soviet Union. Most of Russia's population live west of the Ural Mountains, in the European part, many in the big cities of Moscow and St. Petersburg. Also in this area lies a good part of Russia's farmland, producing cereals and root crops.

East of the Ural mountains is Siberia, a vast area of sparsely populated land. The climate is harsh, with frozen tundra in the north and thick coniferous forest, known as taiga, further south. The deepest lake in the world, Lake Baikal, is found in the south-east. Siberia is rich in coal, oil, gas and metal ores. The region has a small population, but a large number of different peoples.

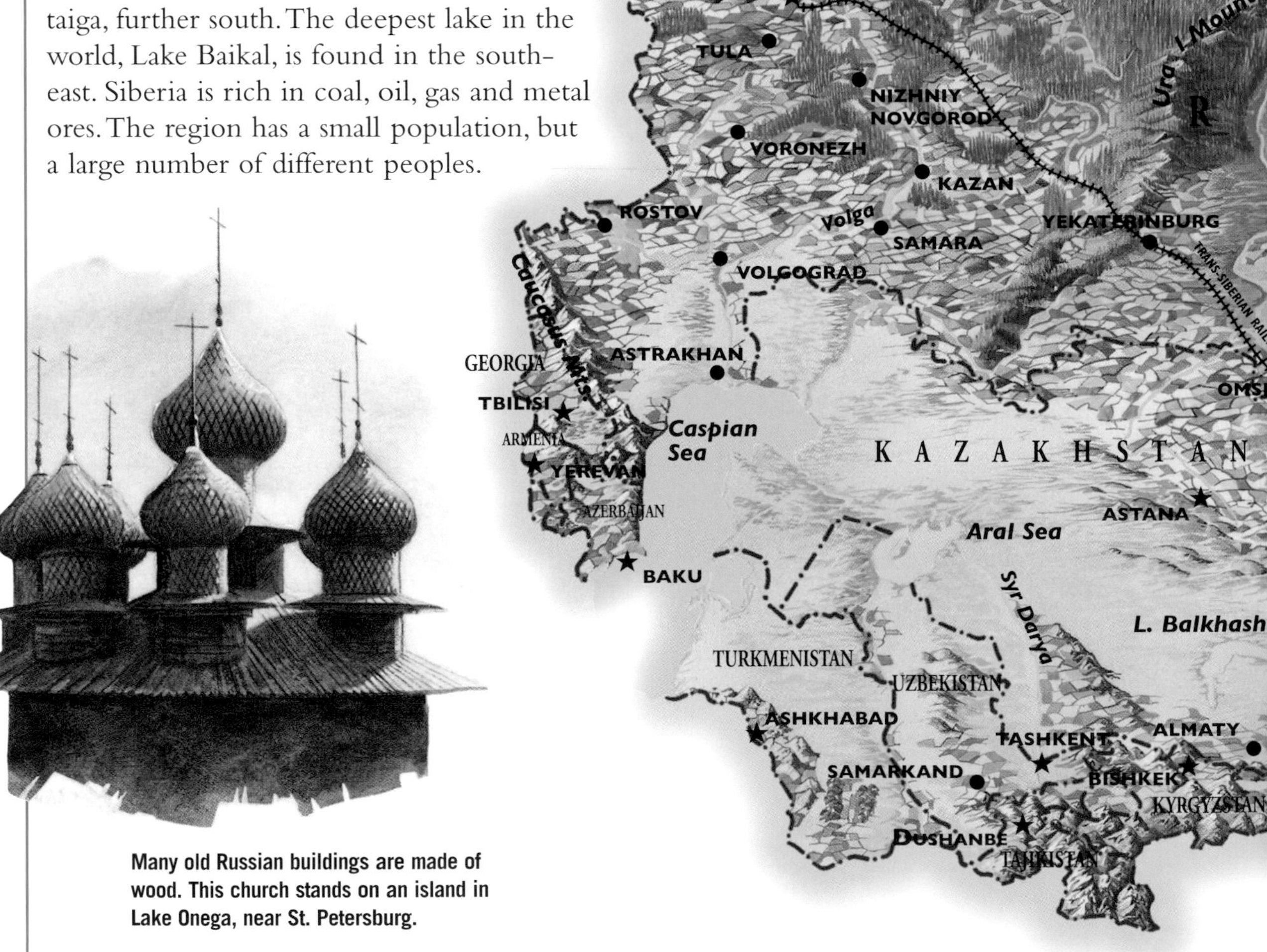

Many old Russian buildings are made of wood. This church stands on an island in Lake Onega, near St. Petersburg.

Scattered around the fringes of the Arctic Ocean are a number of small communities. They herd reindeer or cattle, and use animal skins to keep warm as their ancestors did.

The Trans-Siberian Railway runs from Moscow across the southern part of Siberia. It is a vital link for people and industry between east and west. The longest line in the world, it takes eight days to travel.

Since the collapse of the Soviet Union, Russia, for all its natural mineral wealth, long-established industries and advanced technology, is struggling to develop its economy.

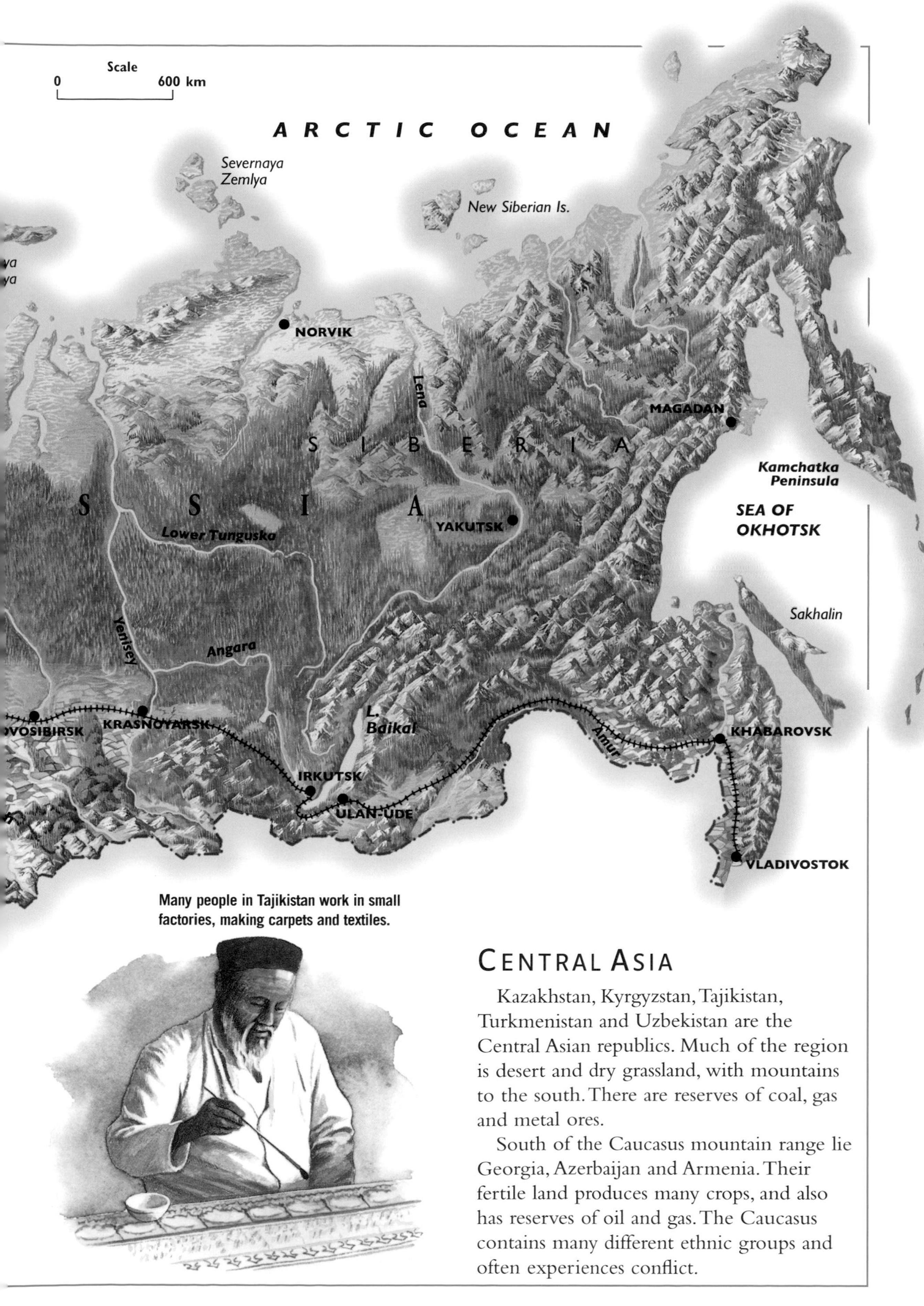

Many people in Tajikistan work in small factories, making carpets and textiles.

Central Asia

Kazakhstan, Kyrgyzstan, Tajikistan, Turkmenistan and Uzbekistan are the Central Asian republics. Much of the region is desert and dry grassland, with mountains to the south. There are reserves of coal, gas and metal ores.

South of the Caucasus mountain range lie Georgia, Azerbaijan and Armenia. Their fertile land produces many crops, and also has reserves of oil and gas. The Caucasus contains many different ethnic groups and often experiences conflict.

MIDDLE EAST

THE COUNTRIES of southwest Asia are known as the Middle East. Much of this region is covered with mountains or desert, and has a hot, dry climate. The most fertile areas are along the Mediterranean coast and the river floodplains of eastern Iraq. Here, crops such as cereals and citrus fruits can be grown.

Other Middle Eastern countries, such as Saudi Arabia, Kuwait and the United Arab Emirates, have become very wealthy despite their lack of water and mostly barren land. They have huge reserves of oil, which they export to the rest of the world.

Some Middle Eastern cities date back thousands of years. Many have a pattern of narrow, winding streets around a central market and mosque for worship. Outside Israel, a Jewish state, most people follow the religion of Islam, but there is also frequent conflict between religious and ethnic groups. Border and territorial disputes between countries have also led to wars in the Middle East.

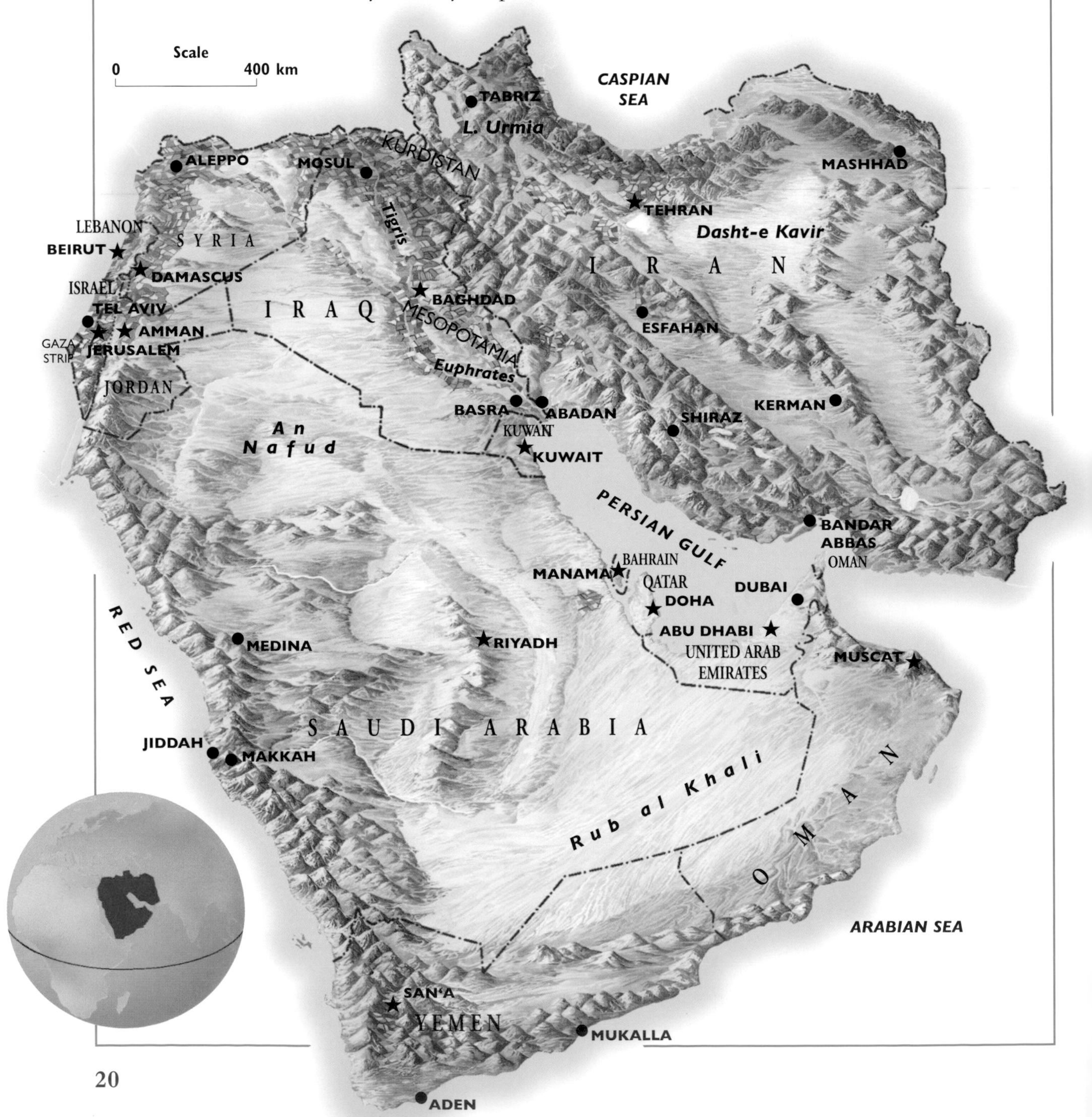

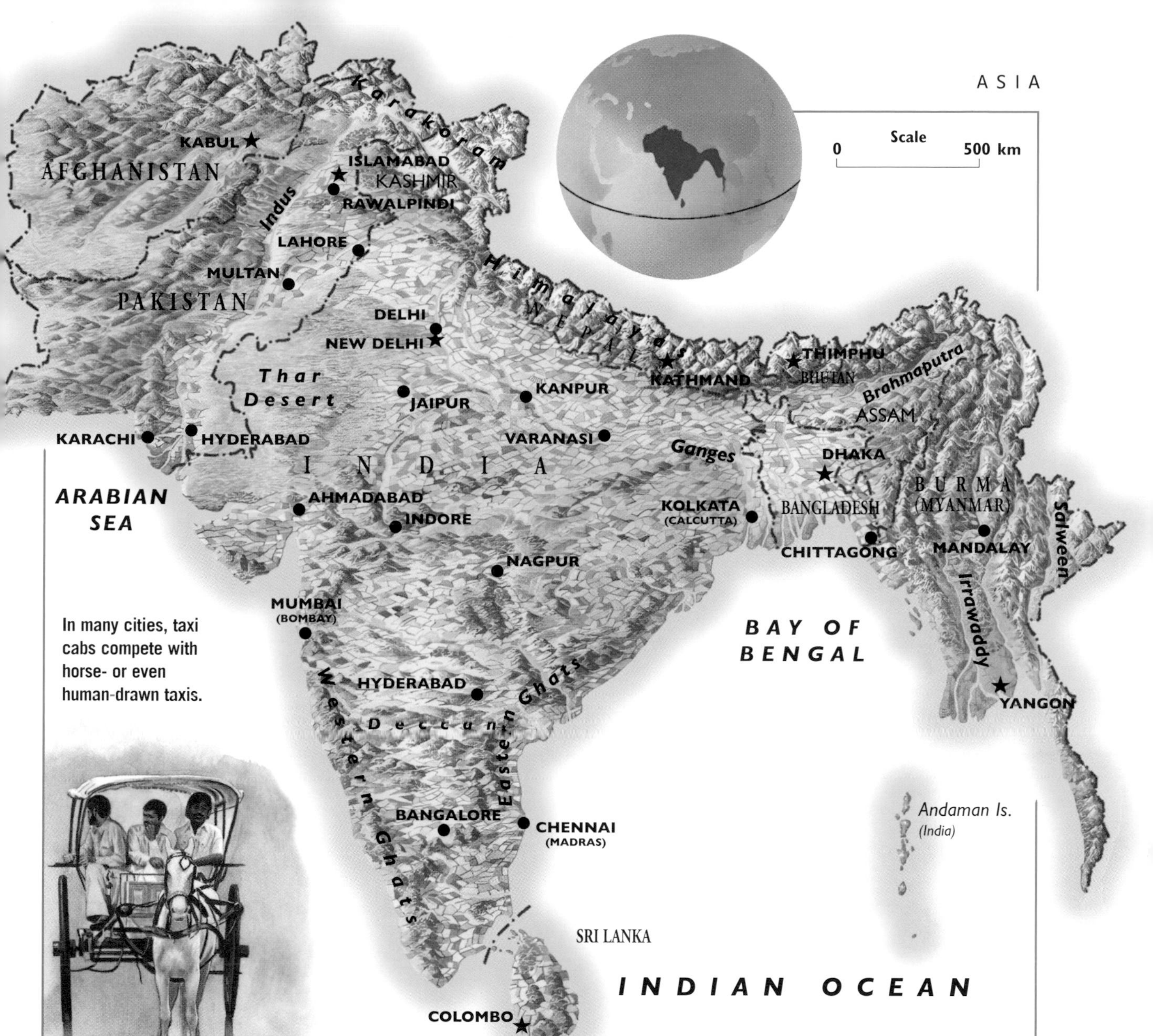

In many cities, taxi cabs compete with horse- or even human-drawn taxis.

SOUTHERN ASIA

THE INDIAN subcontinent encompasses India, Pakistan, Bangladesh, Nepal, Bhutan and Sri Lanka. Much of the northern region is mountainous, with the Himalaya and Karakoram ranges forming a border with the rest of Asia. A region of desert covers eastern Pakistan and northeast India, bordering areas of more fertile land, where farmers grow rice and cotton. The Ganges valley is one of the most intensely cultivated regions in the world. Sri Lanka has large tea plantations, and is a popular tourist resort.

Southern Asia is home to many peoples, with thousands of different languages and several religions. But many people are also very poor. Most are farmers who rely on the monsoon rains to water their crops. They suffer badly when there are droughts or floods, especially in low-lying countries such as Bangladesh. Years of civil war have also added to the poverty in Afghanistan and Burma.

However, some Southern Asian countries are becoming more and more industrialized. India has an important manufacturing industry, producing textiles, clothing and machinery. Its large cities are overcrowded with people who have come from the countryside looking for work.

CHINA

THE THIRD largest country in the world, China also has the highest population—more than one-fifth of all the people in the world today. The west of the country is mountainous, with bleak deserts and grassland plains or steppes. The deserts are freezing cold in winter. The highest point is Mount Everest, which lies on the border between Tibet and Nepal. Tibet used to be an independent country, but has been occupied by China since the 1950s.

In contrast, the eastern part of China has a warm climate, with fertile soil and river valleys. Great rivers, including the Yangtse and the Huang He, or Yellow River, wind their way from the western mountains to the sea. The Grand Canal, the world's longest waterway, stretches for 1790 kilometres. Most of the population of China live in the east. China is a major producer of tea, wheat and sweet potatoes as well as rice, which is grown in the flat, flooded paddyfields of the south. Pigs and poultry are kept everywhere.

Many Chinese cities have populations of more than a million people. Most people live in apartment blocks. China has natural resources such as coal and oil, and also heavy industry such as steel and chemical plants. It is an important producer of textiles, clothing and electronics. Though many people in China are poor, it is a rapidly developing country.

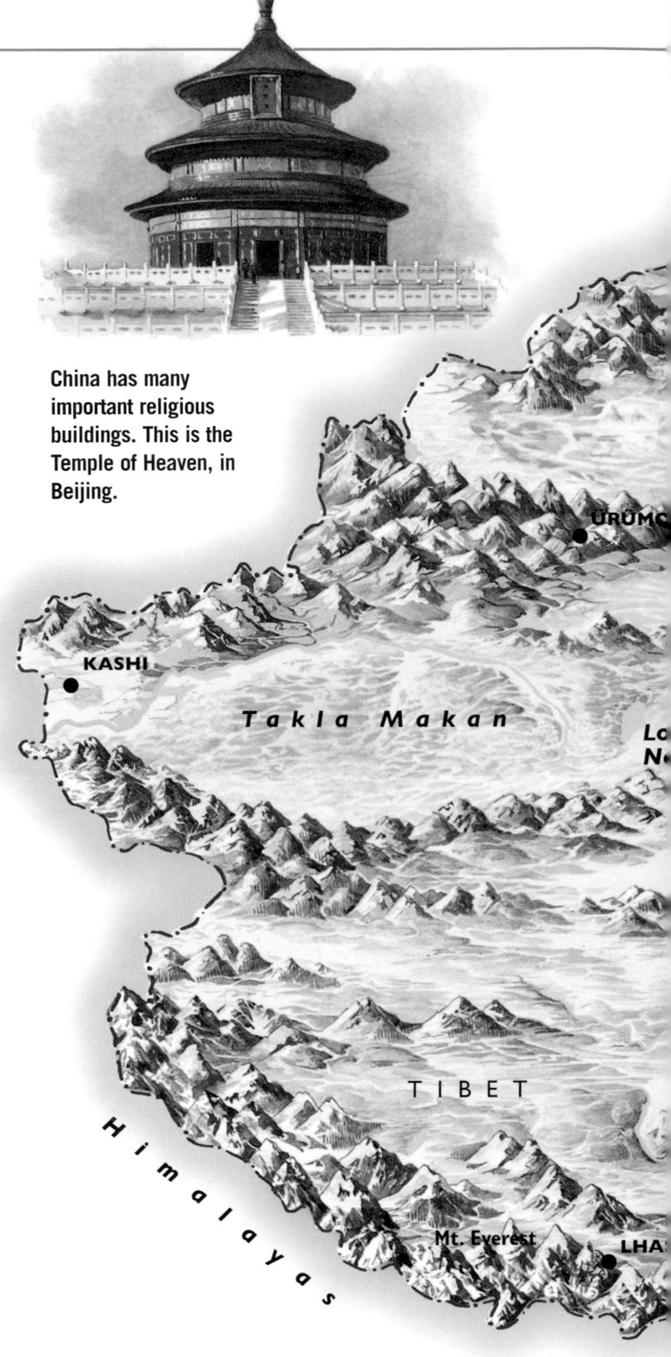

China has many important religious buildings. This is the Temple of Heaven, in Beijing.

Farmers bring their produce into the city markets to sell.

MONGOLIA AND KOREA

Mongolia occupies the grassy plains between the mountains to the north and the Gobi desert to the south. Many people still live a nomadic life on the central plains. Mongolia has coal and oil resources.

North and South Korea are both mountainous and forested, but while North Korea has little contact with the outside world, and relies on enormous state-controlled farms, South Korea has thriving, modern industries and many trade links.

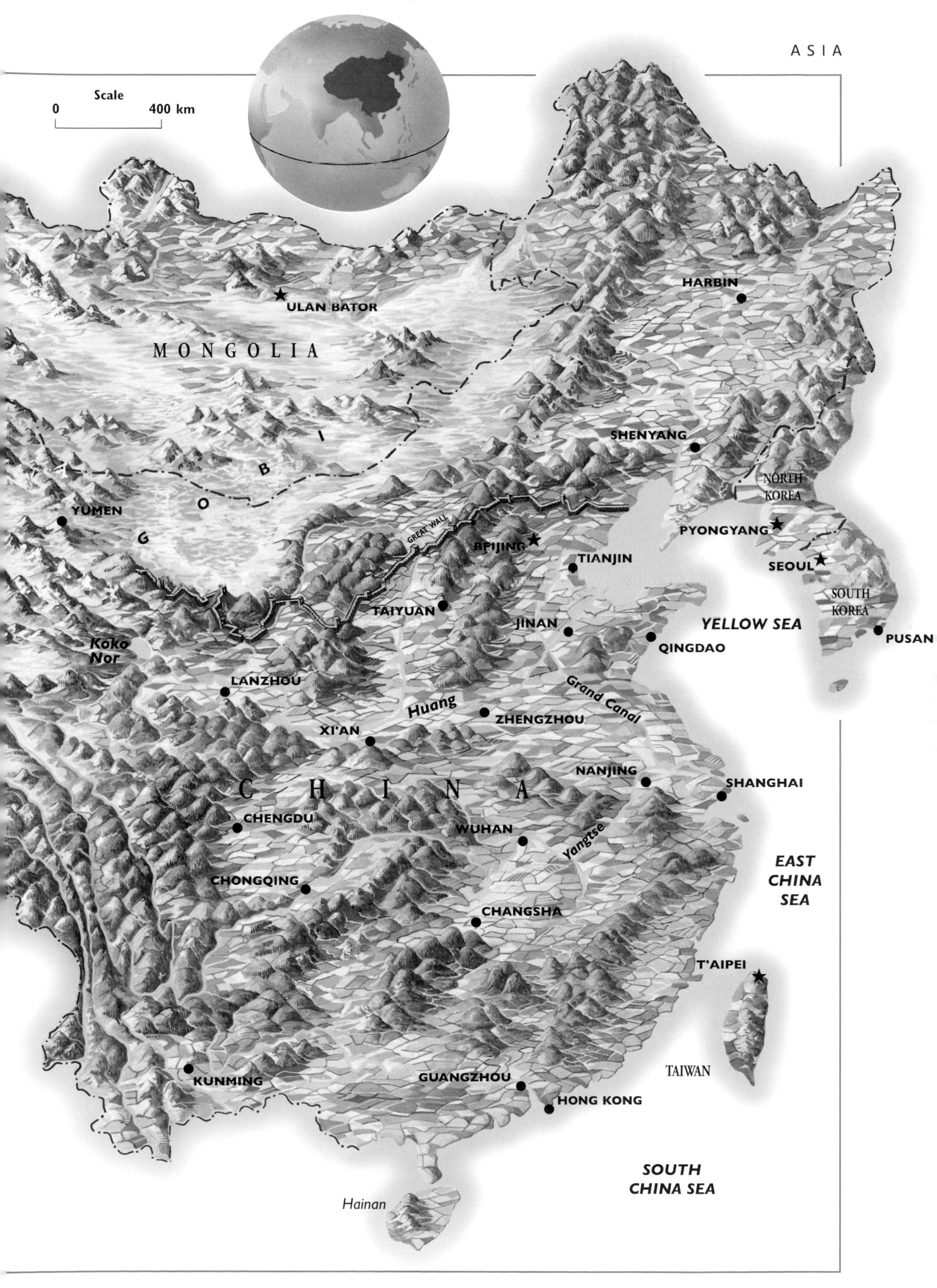

Scale
0
400 km
ULAN BATOR
MONGOLIA
G O B I
YUMEN
GREAT WALL
BEIJING
TIANJIN
HARBIN
SHENYANG
NORTH KOREA
PYONGYANG
SEOUL
SOUTH KOREA
PUSAN
YELLOW SEA
TAIYUAN
JINAN
QINGDAO
Koko Nor
LANZHOU
Huang
Grand Canal
ZHENGZHOU
XI'AN
NANJING
SHANGHAI
CHINA
CHENGDU
WUHAN
Yangtse
EAST CHINA SEA
CHONGQING
CHANGSHA
T'AIPEI
TAIWAN
KUNMING
GUANGZHOU
HONG KONG
SOUTH CHINA SEA
Hainan

Southeast Asia

THE SOUTHEAST corner of mainland Asia, together with thousands of islands further south, make up the region of Southeast Asia. On the mainland are the mountainous, forested countries of Thailand, Laos, Vietnam and Cambodia. Great rivers flow through the region, creating fertile valleys where large quantities of crops such as rice and tropical fruits are grown. Thailand also has successful tourist and manufacturing industries. Cambodia, Vietnam and Laos have been devastated by war, although Vietnam now has a growing industrial economy.

Malaysia is made up of the mainland Malay peninsula, and most of northern Borneo. Southern Borneo, together with other islands including Sumatra and Java, is part of Indonesia. The climate is hot and wet, with areas of dense rainforest that are home to many kinds of plants and animals. Malaysia and Indonesia are rich in natural resources such as oil, gas and rubber. They also have strong manufacturing industries.

North of Borneo are the Philippines, thousands of small islands, many of which are uninhabited. Although their country is rich in mineral resources, many people are obliged to leave to find work in other countries. Both the Philippines and Indonesia are frequently threatened by tropical storms, volcanoes and earthquakes.

The small countries of Singapore and Brunei are among the world's rich countries. While Brunei has huge resources of oil and gas, Singapore is a worldwide centre of manufacturing and business.

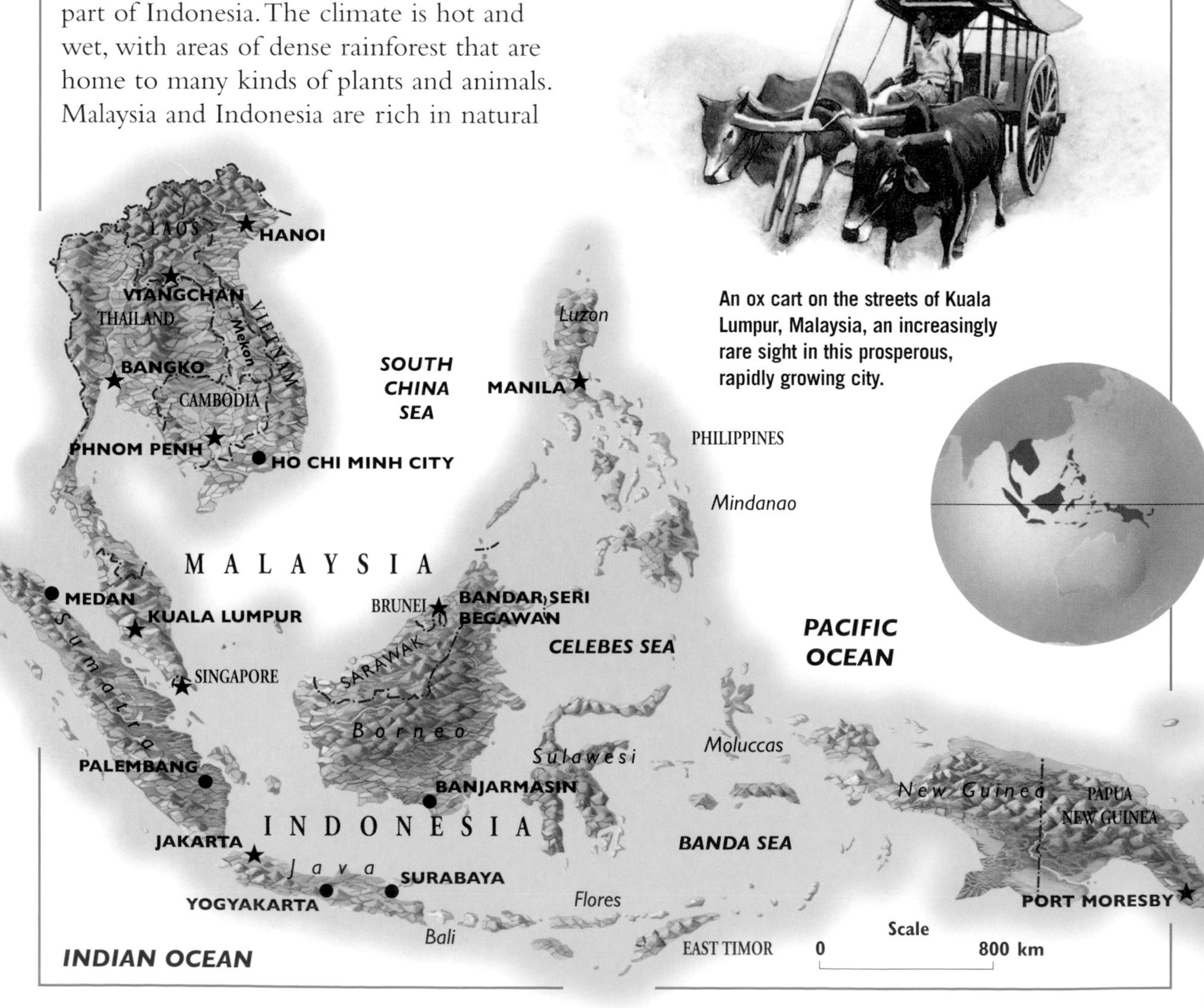

An ox cart on the streets of Kuala Lumpur, Malaysia, an increasingly rare sight in this prosperous, rapidly growing city.

JAPAN

LYING OFF the east coast of mainland Asia, Japan is made up of four large islands, where most of the population live, and thousands of smaller ones. The four main islands are Honshu, Hokkaido, Kyushu and Shikoku. Much of Japan is covered with mountains, some of them volcanic. It is also densely forested. Winter is cold in the north, but the south of the country has mild winters and hot summers.

With limited land available for farming, and a lack of natural resources, Japan has turned to industry and technology for its livelihood. Today, it is a leading producer of cars, ships and electronic goods such as computers, televisions and cameras. It is also a powerful financial centre. Most people live in the cities, several of which have a population of over one million. Their buildings are designed to withstand the earthquakes that frequently occur.

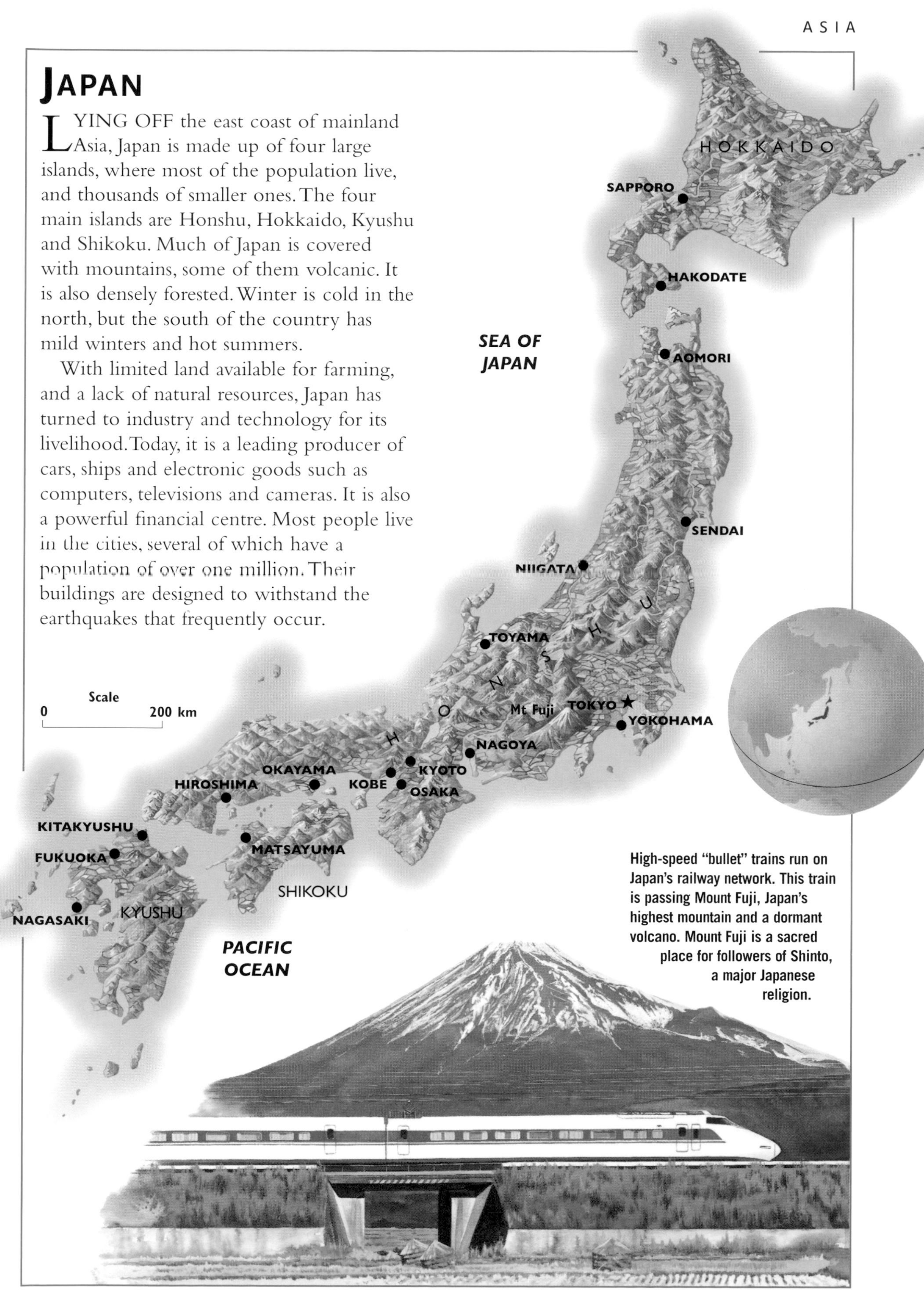

High-speed "bullet" trains run on Japan's railway network. This train is passing Mount Fuji, Japan's highest mountain and a dormant volcano. Mount Fuji is a sacred place for followers of Shinto, a major Japanese religion.

AUSTRALIA

APART FROM a long range of mountains running down its eastern side, most of Australia is flat, hot and dry. It is rich in natural resources such as coal and minerals including gold, copper and iron. The vast interior, or outback, is mostly desert, or dry scrublands. To the east, this

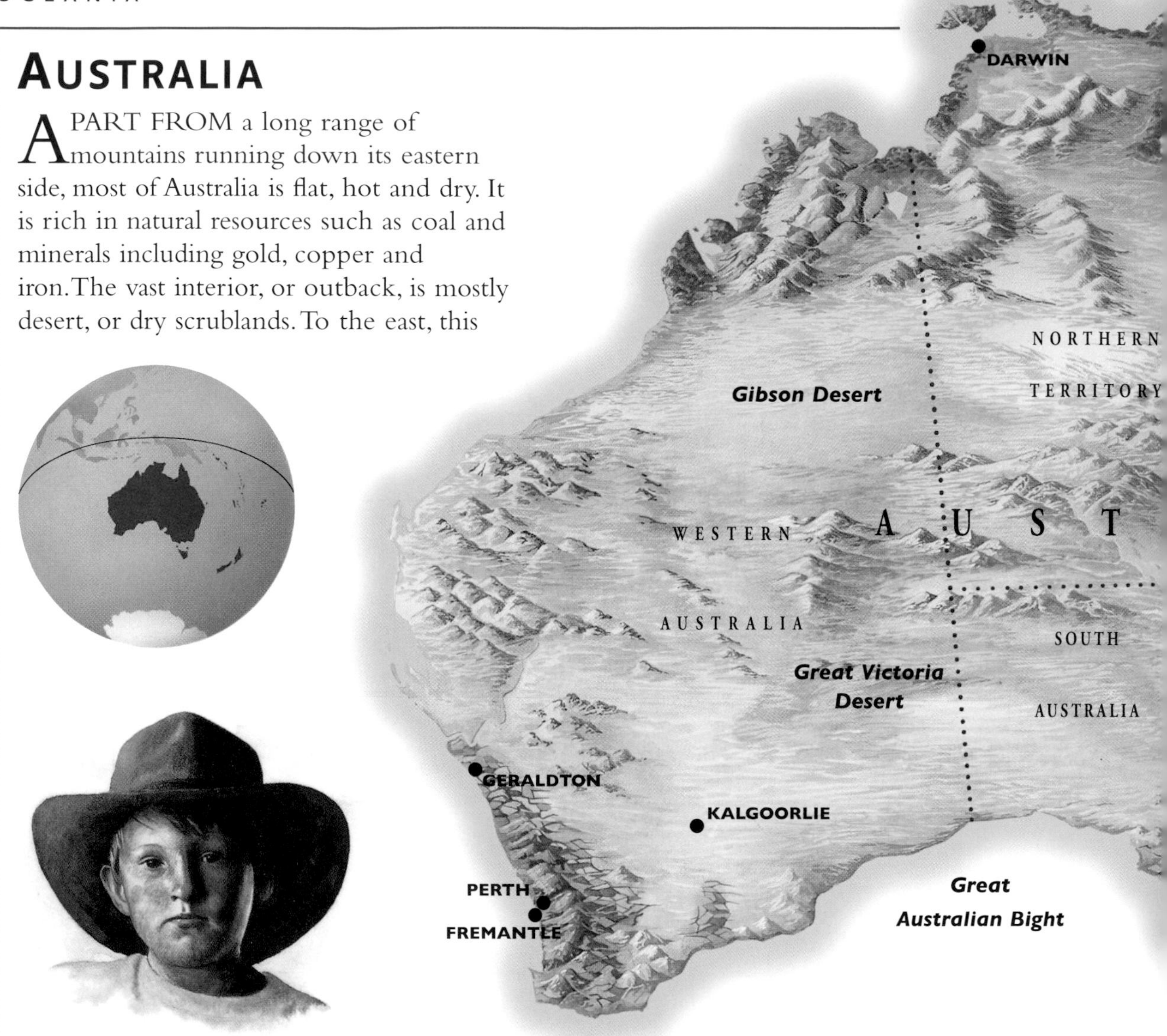

An Australian boy. On the most isolated cattle and sheep stations, far from towns, children must learn their lessons at home. If there is a medical emergency, doctors fly in by aeroplane.

gives way to open grassland—stock-raising country, where Australia's sheep and cattle ranches, or "stations", are situated. With its millions of sheep, Australia is the world's largest producer of wool.

Most Australians live around the coasts, where the climate is cooler and the land fertile. Crops such as wheat and tropical fruits are grown for export, and vineyards produce world-famous wines. A high proportion of people live in the largest cities, such as Sydney, Brisbane and Melbourne. The cities have modern manufacturing industries.

Sydney Harbour Bridge, and the famous Opera House.

About 200 years ago, the British and other Europeans began to arrive on the shores of Australia. They routed many of the native Australians already living there, and seized their land. Today, much of Australia's population is of European descent, although there are substantial numbers of immigrants from Asia. The small number of native Australians that remain are working to reclaim some of their land and sacred sites.

New Zealand is home to several kinds of birds that have lost the ability to fly because of a lack of natural predators. One of these, the kiwi, has become the symbol of New Zealand. Others include the rare takahe *(left)*, which lives in the mountains of South Island.

NEW ZEALAND

Like its neighbour, Australia, New Zealand is a prosperous country. It farms huge numbers of cattle and sheep, producing large quantities of wool, meat and dairy products for export. Its fertile land and warm climate also make it ideal for vineyards and fruit and vegetables. The power of New Zealand's many rivers, and also the underground heat from volcanic activity on North Island, are harnessed through non-polluting electricity schemes.

The native peoples of New Zealand are the Maoris, who originally came from Polynesia. They still make up about nine per cent of the population, and have retained much of their culture and traditions.

New Zealand includes two main islands, North Island and South Island, and several smaller ones. Most people live on North Island.

Northern Africa

THE NORTHERN half of Africa stretches down from the fertile coast bordering the Mediterranean Sea, through vast areas of desert and savanna, into the forests of the west and central Africa. Apart from the Atlas Mountains, the Ethiopian Highlands and Saharan ranges, much of the region is a level plateau.

In the far north of Africa, the countries bordering the coast benefit from natural resources of oil and gas. They also rely on tourism and the manufacture of textiles and carpets. The population are mostly Arabs. Berbers, an ancient native people, live in the uplands of Morocco.

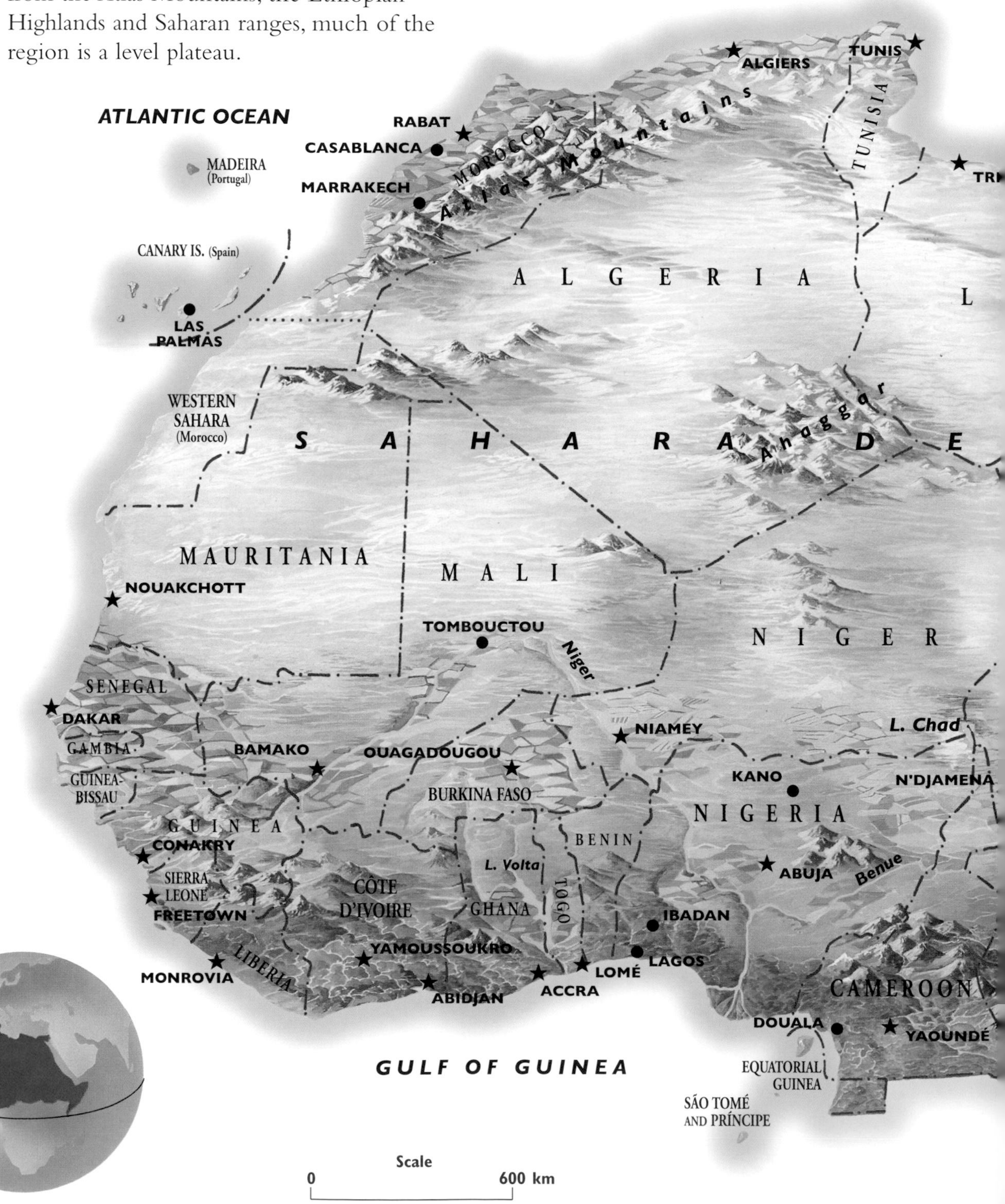

South of the Sahara, agriculture is the primary industry of many countries. Rivers such as the Nile, Niger and Senegal provide essential water with which to irrigate crops. However, in many countries such as Mauritania and Mali, drought is a recurrent problem. In the driest areas, nomadic cattle-herders travel vast distances in search of good grazing.

There are many different peoples living in Northern Africa. Conflict between them often leads to long and devastating wars. The combination of war, drought and widespread poverty has led to terrible famines in Ethiopia and Sudan.

West Africa has a wetter climate, and crops such as coffee, bananas, cocoa, groundnuts and citrus fruits are grown. For many years, timber has been an important product of countries such as the Côte d'Ivoire, but this was carried out at such a rate that vast areas of the forest have now disappeared. Mining of oil and metal ores is a rich resource, but due to poor government and frequent wars, many countries are still impoverished.

Many people in Northern Africa live in small towns or villages, producing just enough food and goods for themselves. Others crowd into the cities, looking for work. They often have to live in very poor conditions on the outskirts of the city.

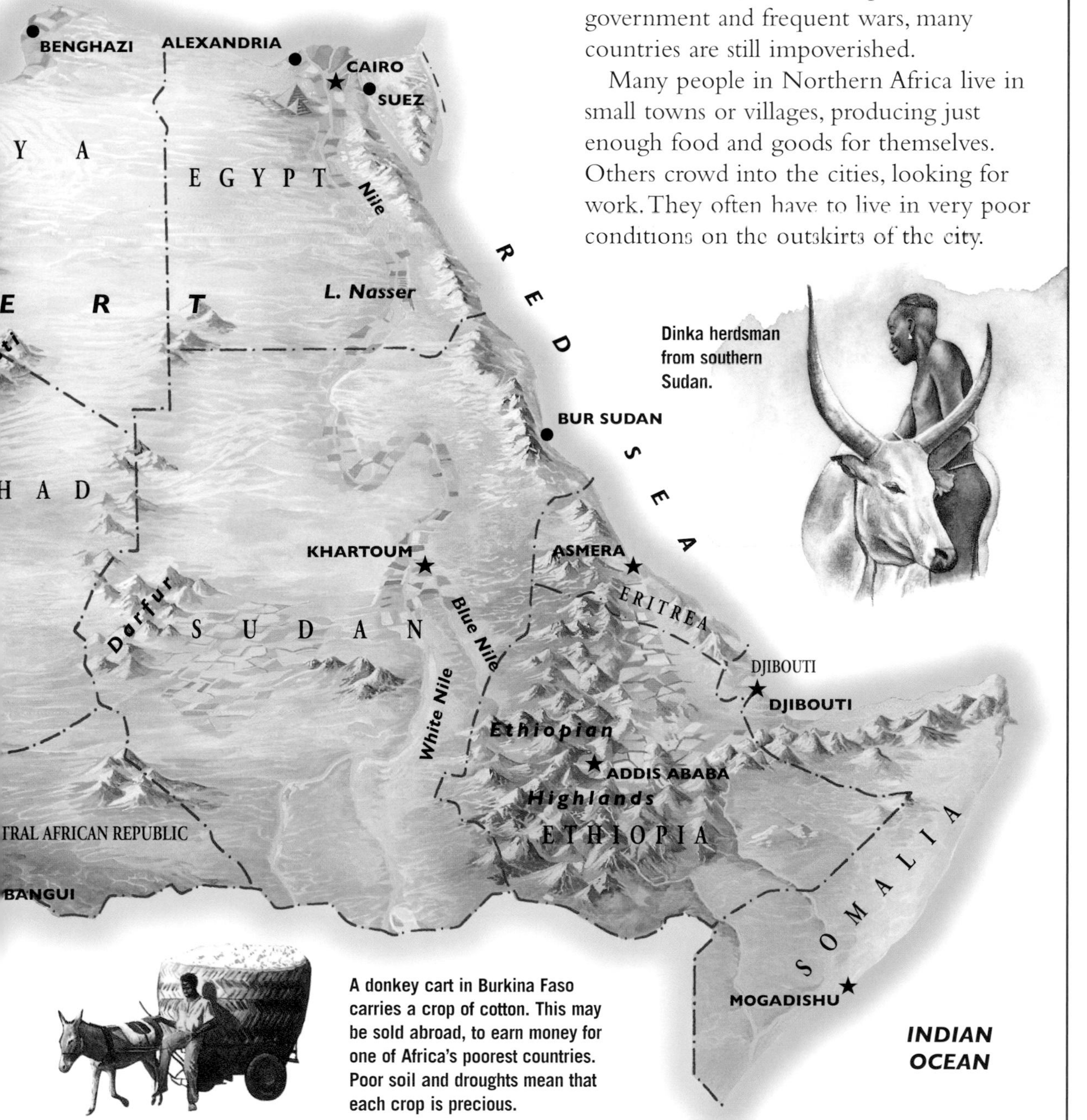

Dinka herdsman from southern Sudan.

A donkey cart in Burkina Faso carries a crop of cotton. This may be sold abroad, to earn money for one of Africa's poorest countries. Poor soil and droughts mean that each crop is precious.

SOUTHERN AFRICA

THE CONGO basin covers much of central Africa. Here, the mighty Congo river winds through dense rainforest, where animals such as the rare mountain gorilla, and a host of bird species live.

To the south and east are high plateaux, with a cooler, drier climate. Much of the land is flat grassland, called savanna, where animals such as giraffes, elephants and lions roam. In the southwest, the savanna gives way to areas of hot, dry desert. In the east, deep valleys, high volcanic mountains and huge lakes have formed along a split in the Earth's crust, known as the Great Rift Valley.

Southern Africa is rich in natural resources such as oil, metals (particularly copper and gold) and diamonds. Mining is therefore a vitally important industry. Tourism is also important to the savanna regions, where large national parks have been set up to protect the wildlife. In the eastern highlands, crops of tea and coffee are grown for export. Cattle are farmed for their meat and dairy products.

This Mozambique woman wears cream made from ground bark on her skin to protect it from the sun. Mozambique was ruled by Portugal until it became independent in 1975.

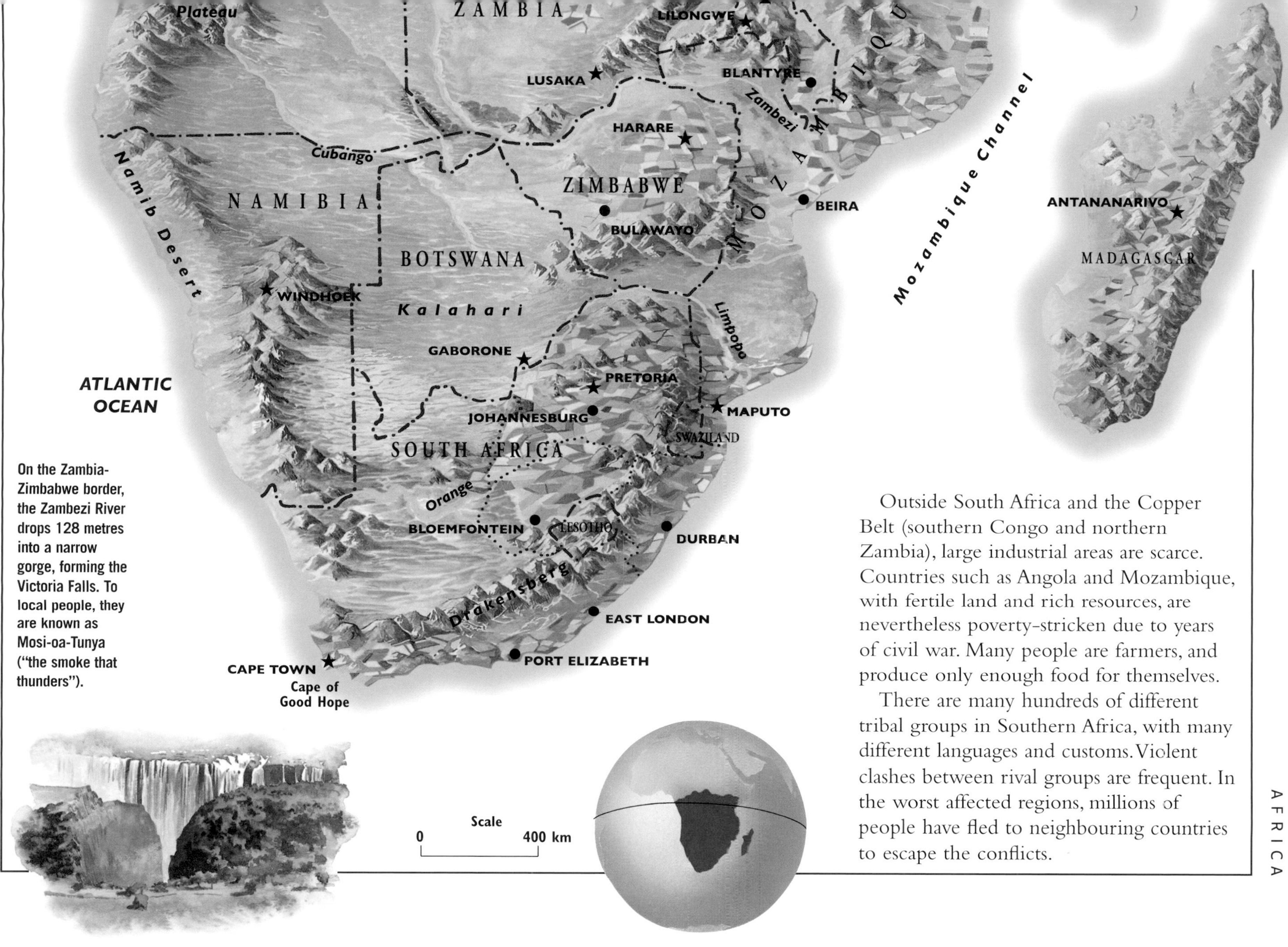

On the Zambia-Zimbabwe border, the Zambezi River drops 128 metres into a narrow gorge, forming the Victoria Falls. To local people, they are known as Mosi-oa-Tunya ("the smoke that thunders").

Outside South Africa and the Copper Belt (southern Congo and northern Zambia), large industrial areas are scarce. Countries such as Angola and Mozambique, with fertile land and rich resources, are nevertheless poverty-stricken due to years of civil war. Many people are farmers, and produce only enough food for themselves.

There are many hundreds of different tribal groups in Southern Africa, with many different languages and customs. Violent clashes between rival groups are frequent. In the worst affected regions, millions of people have fled to neighbouring countries to escape the conflicts.

INDEX